The Borough of

Barnet

Memories

The publishers would like to thank the following companies for their
support in the production of this book

Main Sponsor
Oliver & Saunders Limited

Barnet College

Hendon Police College

The Mount School

Charles Neal & Son (Finchley) Limited

OpTex Limited

Simmonds & Partners

Spires Shopping Centre

Statons Estate Agents

First published in Great Britain by True North Books Limited

England HX5 9AE

Telephone: 01422 377977

Copyright © True North Books Limited, 2000

ISBN 1 903204 16 X

Text, design and origination by True North Books Limited

Printed and bound by The Amadeus Press Limited

The Borough of

Barnet

Memories

Edited by Dr Gillian Gear

Contents

Introduction

I ndulging in nostalgia always brings a warm glow to the senses. We remember life and times that we have lived through and the pleasure they have given us. Sometimes our memory can play tricks. Perhaps it's not quite as accurate as we would like to think. Then there are the moments that are only half recalled. A piece of the jigsaw is missing. Wouldn't it be nice to have something that helps to fill in the gaps or confirm an obscure detail? This is where 'Borough of Barnet *Memories*' can help.

On its own it is a delightful collection of photographs culled from the last century. The captions alongside are a mixture of thought provoking reminiscences, comment and fact. Ally these to the reader's own experience and you have a combination that can roll back the years. Use the book like a time machine, but be prepared to stop off in places that you never realised existed. Get ready to call in on buildings, streets and people your parents told you about. Pass into an era when Barnet folk danced the jitterbug. Travel along the tramlines that once cut through our streets. Thrill again to the passions aroused

by the look of Rudolph Valentino gazing out from the silver screen. In amongst the joy of reliving those days are the sadder moments that must never be forgotten. The 20th century holds so many happy memories, but it also brought pain. There were days when bombs rained down from the skies, smashing our homes to pieces. We had occasions when there was not enough work available to put food on the table for the children. Even as the millennium drew to a close we had rioting in our own cities and civil strife in Ireland. Not everything in the garden was rosy. But, there is so much good to be remembered and 'Borough of Barnet *Memories*' will help you find it.

This publication is not meant to be a history book. It has been compiled both as an addition to the family album and as a work that can stand alone in its own right. Yet to make complete sense of our recent history we must give some thought to times further back. The borough of Barnet may have been born in 1965, but its recorded roots go back hundreds of years. Evidence of Roman civilisation has been found along Watling Street, the road from

A Sunday School group in the 1950s

London northwest via St. Albans (Verulamium) to Wroxeter (Viroconium). Later there were Saxon settlements around the once thickly forested region. The first development of the route that was to become the Great North Road dates to medieval times. But, it was not until the beginning of the 12th century that the world first heard of Barnet as La Barnette or Barneto. Situated on top of a hill, it grew up around the new road, later becoming Chipping Barnet. Chipping is an old word for market. By the end of the century the town had been granted a charter to hold its own market. The famous fair has been held for over 400 years. So well known did it become that Barnet Fair entered the English language as an expression known to far and wide as the rhyming slang for hair. For centuries the outlying district was largely rural, relying on agriculture for its existence, whilst the town relied on its income from travellers and trades associated with horses.

The industrial revolution that transformed parts of Britain that had easy access to iron and coal largely passed it by. Not until the 19th century was there a real explosion in development. The coming of the railway age changed all that. Easy access to and from the outside world turned sleepy towns and villages into thriving satellites of the great metropolis.

But the borough is more than just Chipping Barnet. When the Greater London Council came into being it formed 32 boroughs. Barnet, New Barnet and East Barnet, once in Hertfordshire, joined forces with Middlesex's Friern Barnet, Finchley and Hendon. These districts brought with them their own histories and cultures. Hendon can lay claim to Norman traces in St Mary's, the parish church. There is the famous police training college and impressive RAF museum near the former military airfield.

A charming view of High Street, Barnet c1935.

In the 14th century Hendon was a village that became a refuge from the Black Death sweeping through London. Finchley has Saxon origins. Its name means a wood populated by finches. It can boast of its former moated castle and standing as a major coaching centre in the 18th and early 19th century. At one time 90 long distance coaches rattled through its streets every day of the week.

We have to rely on our history books for information about the past. The facts we know are reliant on the accuracy of the recorder. In 'Borough of Barnet *Memories*' you can make up your own mind. The evidence of your eyes is what is being offered. The camera never lies. We may be selective in what we call to mind, but the image on the photograph is clear. Turning the leaves of the book will provide a rich insight into the borough as it has developed over the 20th century.

Before going to the next page take a little time out to close your eyes and hear the strains of army bands striking up 'It's a long way to Tipperary'. Imagine flappers dancing the Black Bottom or Bing Crosby crooning 'Samantha'. The voice of Vera Lynn will be in there somewhere. Later times will bring back to mind Bill Haley's kiss curl and the pelvis that Elvis gyrated. Open a packet of Spangles and pass round the cups of Ovaltine. With 'Workers' Playtime' on the Light Programme in the background prepare for a journey down memory lane. A tidal wave of nostalgia is about to be unleashed. Put another lump of coal on the fire. Light a Craven A for your throat's sake, as it used to be advertised. Beautiful photographs are about to appear before you. Informative and wry text await you. But, best of all, your nostalgic nodules are about to be reawakened by 'Borough of Barnet *Memories*'.

Events & occasions

Above: On 11 September 1937 the annual horse fair opened on fields just off Barnet Lane. It had moved venues a number of times since first being held on the streets in the 16th century. Elizabeth I in 1588, the year of the Spanish Armada, granted the right for Barnet to hold two fairs each year. Originally they were to be held in June and October as they were linked to saints' days connected with the feasts of St Luke and St John the Baptist. The Common, Chipping Barnet, was regularly used in the 18th and 19th centuries. Horse racing was a popular feature, but cattle were included in the trade as well. Cattle fairs were held in fields off Wood Street until the early 20th century. Some were driven from as far afield as the Scottish Highlands. In the horse fairs large shire horses stood alongside sturdy Welsh ponies as knowledgeable men checked their teeth, withers and hocks. Over the years the noble beasts have been traded at Ravenscroft Park, around Milton Avenue, close to the soccer ground, at Pricklers Hill, Brent Lodge Farm and Mays Lane. The fair has had a colourful and controversial past. The men in the photograph had ignored a council ban on the 1937 fair. The authorities had become more and more concerned that the event was the focal point for crime and civil unrest. Pickpockets and cardsharps moved amongst the crowds. Some dishonest traders used the fair to dispose of stolen horseflesh. Rustling was not just for America's Wild West. There was some of it alive in Hertfordshire. There are still debates about the fair, but it lives on.

Clutching their posies the children were looking forward to their day out at Folly Farm in 1931. Cute faces turned to the camera to record a special occasion for the Sunday School outing that brought them from 'the smoke' to leafy Hadley Woods. They had such a jolly time and talked about it for days afterwards. They came up by train to New Barnet as part of an annual event for the underprivileged of the East End. As part of a demonstration of Christian charity the better off children from Cromer Road School provided the flowers. A decent meal might have been more use. This visit had been organised by St Giles Mission. For 30 years, up to the start of World War II, cheerful children made the journey from the grime of their home surroundings to the open spaces of Folly Farm. The park was a small forerunner of Thorpe Park or Alton Towers. It had swingboats, a steam round-about, a little helter skelter and donkey rides. The attractions were the brainchild of Eli Frusher. He was a local butcher and served the public as a councillor. He bought Folly Farm in 1900, using it to fatten his pigs during the winter before they were sold on at Smithfield Market. He put in fairground rides and equipment as a service for local children. The 17th century house served teas, sometimes using the ham from his own pigs. It was not long before the entertainments were attracting visitors from the inner city. The house was pulled down in 1939 and a housing estate built where the fun had been enjoyed.

Above: The face of Chipping Barnet High Street's west side from Finlay's to the Exchange Buildings of the old Corn Exchange has changed little since the mid 1930s. The retailers have changed and the pace of life quickened, but the scene is immediately recognisable. The tobacconist on the left was a lovely place to linger. Jars of pipe tobacco, racks of briars, cases of cigars and the finest accessories for the discerning smoker were all to be had. Unfortunately, the delightful aromas disguised the damage the products caused. Beautiful and sensuous smells hid the cancer and emphysema that laid customers low before their time. The devil has all the best tunes. He seems to have the best aromas to accompany them. There were other delights that satisfied nasal passages without the same dangers. Crusty loaves, succulent pastries and freshly baked pies made bakeries worth a visit, even if you were not intending to buy. Odorous pizzas, hamburgers and all the other fast foods have now replaced those delicate sensations. They leave a musty smell that seems to hang permanently around every town centre. Roadsweepers should be issued with fragrant sprays as well as brushes to clean up the air in addition to the streets. Note the absence of litter in this photograph. In the 1930s people took their rubbish home with them. They also took memories of warm baps and Balkan Sobranie in their nostrils.

Above right: Pedal power was well to the fore in this mid 1930s view of Barnet's High Street. The camera is pointing north, towards the Exchange Buildings. Car ownership was becoming more popular at this time. The Austin Seven, Morris Cowley, Model Y Ford and Wolseley were just a few of the models that pottered along the roads. Ownership was still largely limited to the purchasing power of the middle classes.

Those less well off used public transport or went under their own steam. Cycling was both a useful means of getting around and a popular pastime. At weekends the lanes were full of cycling clubs and families enjoying day out, bowling along the tree lined Hertfordshire countryside. Before World War II Barnet considered itself to be part of a county near London. It only became one of its suburbs in the latter half of the last century. Even now it is not the administrative centre of the borough that bears its name. Hendon has the town hall, as that building was only opened in 1901. There was much argument in the 1960s about the title that would be taken by the new borough formed by Greater London in 1965. Barnet held sway, but many members of the population still regard themselves as belonging to Hendon, Finchley, Friern Barnet etc first. They are part of the London Borough of Barnet second. Half the residents work outside the borough. A third of these are in managerial or professional positions. The borough is a fairly affluent one. You are more likely to see BMWs than bull nosed Morrises on High Street today.

Right: The coach has unloaded its human cargo. The Barnet UDC wagon is being emptied of the paraphernalia needed to carry out the 1933 ceremony of beating the bounds. All age groups got together to continue the ancient tradition. Now that we are in the third such epoch let us hope that future generations have the same desire to protect the past. It is so easy to scoff at the trappings of heritage. Poking fun is a simple pastime. It usually shows a simple mind. Those who lack any depth in their own lives seem unable to appreciate decent qualities in others. We are in danger of becoming an intolerant society. But without understanding or being knowledgeable about the past how can we make sense of the future? We must not throw out the baby with the bathwater. We have a rich and fascinating history: it must be preserved. Parishioners have been beating the bounds since the 9th century. The custom originated when the parish boundaries were walked and boundary posts checked. There were often disagreements about the accuracy of boundary lines. Neighbouring parishes argued about territorial rights. Their determination to ensure that no encroachment was made could become quite fierce. Thankfully the prickly aspect of the practice became less important. It evolved into a happy and celebratory tradition. That alone is worth preserving. With so much aggro and violence around us in this so-called civilised society we need such occasions.

Below: The costumes worn by those enjoying carnival time in the grounds of Barnet Hospital cannot disguise the era. The women's hairstyles are typical of 1921. The men give the game away. For most of them dressing up was beneath them. It was an age of stiff upper lip and a three piece suit. Fob chains hung from pocket watches neatly stored in waistcoats. Barnet and district Radio Society advertised its existence in the display tent. Similar groups of enthusiasts were springing up across the country. Developments made by Faraday, Hertz and Marconi during the previous century had advanced communication to a state where ordinary individuals could get in touch with one another. Improvements in technology during the first world war helped radio become popular in civvy street as soldiers practised the skills they had learned in the field. As a national venture commercial firms took the first initiatives in British radio after World War I. They regarded broadcasting primarily as point-to-point communications. The British Broadcasting Company Ltd. was established in 1922 as a private corporation under the iron fist of general manager John Reith. The BBC went public in 1927. Although living rooms began to tune in to nationwide broadcasts, amateur hams carried on communicating with each other from their personal sets. They provided the inspiration for a hilarious sketch by Tony Hancock, the popular comedian of the 1950s and 1960s. He had his fans in tucks when he tried to follow up a Mayday distress call.

The war memorial used to stand on High Street, near the corner to the narrow stretch of road known as the Squeeze. It was erected in 1922. Field Marshal Viscount Byng of Vimy conducted the service of dedication. He had commanded the Third Army in World War I and was later to become Governor General of Canada and the Commissioner of the Metropolitan Police. He was a descendant of the Byng family of Wrotham Park. Admiral John Byng, son of Sir George Byng, bought the estate in 1750. In 1928 huge crowds gathered on Armistice Sunday to pay their respects to those sons and daughters of Barnet who had died in the Great War. Wreaths were laid in their honour. Heads were bared and bowed. Many an ex-serviceman shed a tear for those pals left behind in the poppy fields of Europe. Women still grieved for the sons and husbands lost in the Flanders mud. The nation vowed never again to allow itself to be involved in a war that would cost the lives of nearly 1,000,000 members of the British Empire. The promise was broken by the end of the next decade. The war memorial was moved into St John the Baptist's churchyard in 1937. This was to help the new trolley bus service operate more freely. The powers-that-be gave more importance to the comfort of paying passengers than they did to acknowledging the sacrifice of the fallen. 'Lest we forget', the memorial service says.

Left: Crescent Road is off East Barnet Road, between New Barnet and Cockfosters. However, the geography is not important. This could be a back street in Glasgow, a road in Newcastle or on an estate in Southampton. The site has no significance. The event meant everything. Across the nation the same scene was being repeated in every street. The long, dark days of the second world war had drawn to a close. By now the children in the party hats, faces swathed in smiles, will be thinking about applying for their bus passes before too long. In 1945 they were excited about the chance of seeing dad again. He would soon be on his way home. Mums and sweethearts waited anxiously for that day to dawn. For some there would be no homecoming. But, those left widowed or fatherless did not let their sadness spoil the day. They celebrated the greater good that the news from the Far East had brought. In May the war in Europe had ended. People had partied then. Now it was time to let their hair down once more. Trestle tables were snaffled from schools and church halls. Jellies, fancies and meat paste sandwiches adorned the tablecloths. Jugs of lemonade were passed round. Ration books were emptied of coupons in a good cause. On 14 August the Emperor of Japan surrendered and VJ Day began in the early hours. Ships' sirens and railway train whistles woke the sleeping population as two days' of national rejoicing began.

Above: The jubilee celebrations for George V took many forms. Standard Telephones and Cables decided to mark the occasion with a formal dinner. It was held in the works' canteen at New Southgate. Flags and bunting hung above the heads of the diners. On the wall were pictures of the King and Queen Mary. She was the only daughter of Prince Herzog of Teck. She had been engaged to George's brother, but he died a few weeks before the marriage should have taken place. Mary married her husband in 1893. She was well known for her fashion sense, invariably appearing wearing a handsome toque as a headdress. The canteen that was the dinner venue normally held workers in overalls and clerks in business suits. But the occasion was too momentous for casual wear. The last time Britain celebrated a monarch's silver jubilee had been in 1862. No one here could remember that day. So, they got the dinner suits out of mothballs. The women went shopping for elegant dresses. They could not possibly wear something that had been seen before. When they sat down at table they nodded approvingly at the table decorations and scanned the wine list. The company chairman made a fine rousing speech. It was good to be British. Other countries had their presidents and chancellors. We had a monarchy and we knew which we preferred. Glasses were raised as the whole canteen stood to make the loyal toast. God save the King.

THE BOROUGH OF BARNET *Memories*

olly Farm stood on the edge of Hadley Woods. It was a popular place for city folk to come and get a bit of rural life for the day before returning to the grime of the capital. They could wander through the woods and stroll in the countryside that seemed a different world to people whose daily existence was surrounded by street upon

street and row upon row of housing. When they tired of walking they could be entertained on the fairground rounds that were built here in the early 1900s. Before returning home they refreshed themselves by taking tea and sandwiches in a delightful setting. They were often told tales about one of the farm's previous owners. Thomas Turpin lived here c 1680. Locals

amused themselves by assuring gullible city dwellers that he was related to the infamous highwayman, Dick Turpin. The notorious villain was born in Hampstead, but, after some dirty dealings in Essex, he went north. Still, it made a good tale. This scene from 1931 shows Folly Farm at the height of its popularity. Displays and marching bands often provided a diversion from the swingboats and donkey rides. This brigade proudly showed off its colours as it strode forward to the beat of the snares and bass drum. Within a decade some of them would be marching off under another set of colours belonging to a regiment crossing the Channel to engage the enemy. When they returned Folly Farm gave way to a housing estate of 1,200 homes, a school and a park.

Right: In November 1939 the war was still a novelty. The British Expeditionary Force was in France and, although some of our shipping had fallen victim to the U-boats, it remained likely that it would be all over by Christmas.

Below: Mrs Montague was giving these lads some words of wisdom from her promotional caravan at the end of road safety week on 20 October 1953. They needed to listen carefully. As car

People had short memories. They said the same thing in 1914. The 1st New Barnet Company of the Boys' Brigade of Brothers had a balancing act to carry out. The aim of the brigade was to 'advance Christ's kingdom amongst boys'. How did that fit with killing Germans? They were Christians. Amongst older members there was a lot of discussion about what could be classified as a just war. The Boys' Brigade still flourishes as a worthwhile society for lads to join. In the London District of Brigades over 50 companies meet in regular communal ceremonies. The movement was started in 1883 by William Smith, a Glasgow mission hall Sunday School teacher. Within three years the Victorian desire to promote goodness in its youth saw 2,000 join the ranks, from Ayr to Inverness. It soon filtered down to London and was well established in Ireland by 1890. The Duke of York, later King George V, was the Brigade's patron for 40 years. Camping became a regular pursuit, out in what Smith, a city man, called 'the wilds'. The annual display of 1903 was held at the Royal Albert Hall, attended by General Baden-Powell. It provided him with the inspiration to found the Scout movement. William Smith was knighted for his services in 1909. He died in 1914, the year after the Brigade's golden jubilee.

ownership was on the increase the number of accidents spiralled. Youngsters were particularly at risk. Children had once played football in the street without a care in the world. They crossed roads after the war on their way to school without too much bother. Petrol rationing kept traffic to a minimum. As restrictions were lifted and people had more money to spend when the austere years were left behind, the motor car became a more frequent sight. The publicity machine rolled into action. Little ones were given lessons in looking right, left and right again. They were told not to cross near parked cars and encouraged to use pedestrian crossings. The Highway Code became their Bible. In later years there would be further attempts to keep our children safe. Along came the cycling proficiency scheme. There was the Tufty Club and the rather odd looking man who encouraged kids to use the Green Cross Code. The youngsters listening to Mrs Montague half a century ago will now be in their 50s. Do they recognise themselves in their school uniforms? Their children will be amused to see those little caps. Boys did not think them hysterically funny. They were just what they were expected to wear.

unions responsible for workhouses. Under the new law, all relief to the able-bodied in their own homes was forbidden. All who wished to receive aid had to live in the institutions. Conditions in the workhouses were deliberately harsh and degrading in order to discourage the poor from relying on parish relief. Barnet Union was formed at a meeting in the Red Lion on 4 July 1835. This orphanage gave children a building where they could live, but it never felt like home. Charles Dickens described this sort of establishment well in 'Oliver Twist'.

Top: You might be forgiven for instantly recognising these pretty young women as Land Army girls. You would be wrong. They were members of the Kentish Town Young Farmers' Club. There were Land Army girls around in 1943, but these women had been brought up as true daughters of the soil. They were attending Hendon Show and were obviously enjoying both the occasion and the sunny weather. The crops ripening in the fields would have been happy with the cloudless sky as well. The club members wore riding breeches and jodhpurs as if they born to them. They looked perfectly natural because theirs was a life on the farm. Strong but tender fingers milked cows. Horses were mounted as easily as getting on a bus. Eggs were collected and cereal crops gathered with an experience gained from involvement since they could toddle. When the Land Army girls were conscripted or volunteered to work on the farms these young farmers often introduced them to their new roles. Puzzled frowns on faces meeting an udder for the first time were soon smoothed away as the women in the photograph demonstrated the way to ease milk into the pail. They could not do much about aching backs and roughened hands. Only a warm bath and plenty of hard work would help them come to terms with tough and demanding labour.

Above: Trams first ran in the borough in 1904. This one was on its way towards the parish church in Barnet, passing the celebratory parade as it clanked its way along the tracks that scarred the streets for much of the first half of the 20th century. The handsome building at 27 High Street was Guyscliffe House. It was only demolished c 1997. Accommodation for Barnet College can now be found here. It had been the Barnet Union Children's Home. Our Victorian ancestors had a mixture of charity and severity in their makeup. In 1835 the Poor Law Reform Act outlawed the employment of children under nine in mills and factories. Paupers and orphans were to be provided for by the state. This was a noble enterprise. In practice, though, it continued the role of the workhouse. People who would have perished on the streets were brought inside to live and work. Their lives were saved, but the conditions were harsh. It was not just the needy who lived there. Workhouses became dumping grounds for criminals, social misfits and the mentally ill. The 1835 act tried to address some of the problems, but only succeeded in part. Groups of parishes were combined into

Little tots in tutus and ballet shoes followed the brightly decorated float along Station Road. Whit Monday in June 1949 dawned bright and sunny. The lorry's engine had fired first time without the need to use the old starting handle poking out from the front. It was a perfect start for the carnival. Hair was ribboned or plaited. Dresses were carefully ironed and little faces smartly scrubbed. The carnival queen mounted her throne on the back of the lorry. She wore her sash proudly and waved to the crowds lining the streets. Her assistants and handmaidens looked beautiful in their long gowns. If one of them felt a pang of jealousy that she had not been given the top honour, then her public face kept it hidden. What she said in private might have been different! Taking part in the Whit walk was a good excuse for showing off. Traditionally, children got new clothes. They almost sparkled as they strode smartly along the road. It was also an occasion to visit aunts and uncles whom they had not seen for 12 months. The relatives gave the children shiny shillings as gifts when they came to call. They knew that they were unlikely to see them again until next year. Some breathed a sigh of relief! Others just accepted it as part of normal family life. They only came to visit when they wanted something for nothing. A friend in need is a friend indeed. A relative in need is a blessed nuisance!

The 25th year of the reign of George V was marked in a variety of ways. There were parties in the streets. A carnival atmosphere was hung over the festivities in the parks. Bands played and speeches were made. The quadrangle in front of the classrooms of the former Queen Elizabeth Boys' Grammar School echoed to the sound of a hundred voices. Conducted by CW Harris, the choir went through its harmonious repertoire, finishing, naturally enough, with the National Anthem. Sadly, the sentiments fell on deaf ears as God did not save the King for another anniversary. The different voice pitches collected in little knots, their places indicated on the boards. Sopranos lilted to the high notes as the resonant bass baritones provided the foundation to each melody. They were gathered under the school's famous mulberry tree. The school was originally housed in the old Tudor Hall, Wood Street. On 24 March 1573 Elizabeth I granted a charter permitting Barnet to open a 'common grammar school'. It was known as free education. The description meant that the church did not control it. Fees still had to be paid. Exactly 300 years later it was given endowed status. Although classroom blocks were added in later years next to the Tudor Hall, by 1932 it was decided to move into more modern premises in Queens Road. Some of the students returned to their alma mater to take their places in the choir. The school went comprehensive in 1971.

Below: It was as far back as 1848 that Karl Marx and Fredreich Engels published the 'Communist Manifesto', a pamphlet of socialist doctrine that was to affect world politics on a large scale in the 20th century. The days of the oppressive ruling classes were numbered in Russia in the early 1900s. The poverty and pain created by the first world war helped the 1917 revolution succeed where that in 1905 had only limited success. Other countries took note. When governments failed to deliver the prosperity they had promised socialists and communists prospered. The equally vocal fascists adopted a radically opposed, but equally volatile, stance. Civil war in Spain followed in the 1930s. At home the Communist Party, led by Harry Pollitt, its general secretary, followed the lead of such notable union figures as Tom Mann. They took to the streets in protest at high unemployment and low wages. Their targets were the fat cats of industry and government. The march in Finchley, on May Day 1939, demanded equality for the working classes. One way forward was through better education for their children. One of the banners made the point. Free the mind and the bodies can escape from persecution, the message seemed to imply. The marchers would be partly pacified by RA Butler's Education Bill in 1944 that introduced free secondary education not dependent on a means test and raised the school leaving age to 15.

Bottom: It was ironic that the USSR, then the world's largest communist country, was to become our ally during the second world war. A few months before hostilities broke out Finchley United May Day Committee, a branch of the British Communist Party, took to the streets. Load hailers on the tops of private cars urged workers to unite against their capitalist masters. The appalling living conditions in the East End of London provided the Communist Party with many sympathisers. Amongst their sworn enemies was Sir Oswald Mosley, a former cabinet minister and founder of the New Party in 1931. This developed into the British Union of Fascists.

Pitched street battles between the blackshirts of the BUF and Communist Party supporters were a regular feature of rallies in the late 1930s. Mosley was interned in May 1940 as he had 'associations with the enemy'. In January 1941 the government would become increasingly concerned about the actions of Communist Party activists. They were accused of handing out leaflets telling people that the air raids were just a plot for capitalists to damage homes and make more profits for themselves. The party's newspaper, the Daily Worker, was banned, though this was lifted in August 1942 as the Germans closed in on Stalingrad. Mosley was released from prison in November 1943. He was still preaching his anti-semitic and racist views in London in 1962. He died in 1980 before he had chance to see the political changes in East Germany and the USSR.

I t was not all fun and jollity during the days of celebration when Queen Elizabeth was crowned as head of the United Kingdom and the Commonwealth. She was also taking on the role as titular head of the Church of England. The abbreviation FD appears on all our coinage. It refers to the title Fidei Defensor (Defender of the Faith) awarded to Henry VIII in the 1520s. It was only right and proper that church services should be held to mark the momentous day. After all, our national anthem is 'God save the Queen'. Two processions made their way into the grounds of Avenue House. They joined in an open air service led by the Anglican and Free Churches. Members of other faiths forgot their differences and joined in the prayers and hymn singing. The 2,500 congregation sang the National Anthem as a hymn at the start of the service of dedication. The Bishop of Willesden gave the address and a 500 strong choir raised its collective voice in celebration. People who never saw the inside of a church from one year to the next were also drawn to the lower lawns of Avenue House by the sense of occasion. There is always something that nags at the conscience of people who are not churchgoers. They have no time for religion, but are first in the queue when it comes to a church wedding, christening or funeral. Perhaps they are hedging their bets!

Below: Pretty girls always turn a man's head, no matter what age he is. This lovely trio, although focused on the camera, was well aware of the effect it was having on the men they were driving past. Women have a sixth sense that lets them know when they are under scrutiny. They also have eyes in the back of their heads. So, if the fellow sneaking an admiring glance thought he was getting away with it, think again. If the lady behind him were his wife she would have noticed as well. There was trouble in store when he got back! But, it would have been worth it. This bevy of beauty was worth a second glance. Diane Potter, from East End Road, was a tender 18 year old and Finchley's Carnival Princess. She was attended by the blonde Kathleen Theodas, age 20, of Avondale Avenue and 17 year old Dorothy Keane from Holdhurst Avenue. If they have any grandchildren by now they can look at granny the next time she comes to call and say, 'My goodness, you were a stunner!' The trio was taking part in the celebrations for the 1953 coronation of Queen Elizabeth II. They were riding in an open topped American car, owned by two GIs. If the youngsters ask their grandmothers how well they knew the servicemen they will get a smile and no proper answer. Every girl likes to keep a sense of mystique about her, even when there is nothing to tell. Gran can still keep grandpa on his toes.

Above: Boys and girls adopted different poses when watching the aerobatics at Hendon Aerodrome. The male of the species could not take his eyes off the magnificent machines that spiralled, dived and pulled up towards the clouds above their heads. Binoculars were trained in their direction. Knowledgeable types showed off their encyclopaedic awareness of engine speeds, horsepower and aircraft makes. Is it any wonder that generations of little lads bought comics then and in later days to read about the exploits of air aces? The incomparable Braddock and Rockfist Rogan, the scourge of the Hun, became required reading material for every red-blooded youngster. The girls could stick to Film Fun. The body language of the young women during the air display suggests that they would have been happier at a gymkhana. Dad had said they would enjoy the aeroplanes. Tell that to the one with her arms folded in that perfect display of feminine disinterest. Perhaps when the pilots stepped out of their planes they might have perked up. In the meantime they could always poke fun at the caps that even teenaged lads had to wear as part of their uniform. Any prefect spotting a student going around without his cap would have him fagging for him for a week. It was really a shame. How could anyone feel anything but self conscious in such headgear? He could hardly compete with the manliness of the flying helmet worn by Hendon's equivalent of Biggles.

Right: When this photograph was taken there were still several hours of entertainment to be had before the long trek home from Hendon's 1937 air show. Before World War I there had been a few air races and some public flying at Hendon. But, it was in 1919 that the first full season of flying took place. A Victory Aerial Derby was held in June with the RAF Pageant taking place in 1920. In between the wars there were many such events. While crowds were getting used to seeing pilots demonstrate their skills in the skies above North London, they saw them for real during World War II. The Battle of Britain was fought before the very eyes of people who used to thrill at the mock battles enacted for them. By the time war was declared most of the fighter squadrons had moved to other fields, though other squadrons used it for short periods. Only 24 Squadron stayed at Hendon. Transport units were concentrated here instead, serving the RAF and the American Air Force. The airfield's runways had to be strengthened and increased to accommodate the heavier loads these aircraft carried. Air displays resumed in 1945. By then jet aircraft were the planes of the future. The last RAF unit left in 1957. The final landing on Hendon's runway took place in 1968 when a Blackburn Beverley put down. RAF Hendon officially closed in 1987. The impressive RAF Museum is now based there.

STAND FULL

Above: You hardly need the sign to tell you that there is not a seat to be had. Even so, the aerobatic displays at Hendon air show were so thrilling that people leapt to their feet in excitement. When has a soccer crowd ever sat down to celebrate a goalmouth incident or stayed still to applaud a home side's goal? Even the committee, who just had to have its own entrance to show off its importance, could not contain itself. The 1937 display was of interest to people other than the general public. Representatives of foreign governments could be numbered among its ranks. No doubt they were making notes for future reference. Ordinary citizens watched with amazement as vapour trails criss-crossed the sky. Loop the loops and barrel rolls kept them engrossed. The skilful way in which aircraft flew in and out of one another was fascinating. The overseas dignitaries took more notice of the last item on the agenda. A mock raid on a small port was staged. Despite the best efforts of anti aircraft gunners, barrage balloons and the finest fighter defences, the battle was lost. The attacking force of bombers, that included Wellesleys and Blenheims, pounded 'Port Hendon' to destruction.

Above right: On the Saturday before the Coronation 200 adults and 80 children form Long Lane, East Finchley attended a party held at Alder School. They blew up balloons, hung streamers across the school hall and held a fancy dress competition. Crowns and coronets were much in evidence, but some tried to be a little different in their choice of costume. However, it was difficult to tell whether the lads in bowler hats were pretending to be Charlie Chaplin or a thin version of Oliver Hardy! Not that it mattered. It was important that they had fun. When children and adults join together to hold a party then laughter is guaranteed. The grown ups let their hair down without any inhibitions as they become just big kids once again. Why else did dad put on short trousers and dig out his old school blazer and cap? They were all there, from toddlers to 70 somethings. Most lived in the area between Brighton Road and the Dick Turpin pub. They played musical chairs and feasted on the buns and cakes they had brought with them as a contribution to the refreshment table. The party was put on at a cost of £70, which helped provide every youngster with a coronation cup, saucer and plate. Older children received a propelling pencil. Mantelpieces all over the country would be adorned with mugs showing a picture of the Queen for years to come. Adults put on a cabaret that showed many hidden talents. Mrs Kathleen Small received her prize in the fancy dress competition from Alderman and Mrs HH Wilmot, but everyone was a winner that day.

Below: East Barnet was still an urban district of Hertfordshire on 9 February 1952. Three days before this crowd gathered King George VI had died. His elder daughter, Elizabeth Alexandra Mary, succeeded to the throne. She returned from a safari in Kenya to find proclamations of her monarchy being read at town halls across the land. East Barnet residents braved the winter chill to listen to the reading of the formal statement. The standards were lowered to half mast in respect. The building in front of the new queen's subjects was designed by Frederick Shenton. It opened in June 1892. The district had been administered by the 1873 East Barnet Valley Board. Control passed to East Barnet UDC in 1894 and it continued to hold the reins until the merger into a London borough in 1965. The town hall was sold in 1988. It became a restaurant in 1996. Perhaps some of the younger members of the crowd now dine at the building outside which they stood half a century ago. As they listened to the proclamation being made they must have wished that the new monarch would bring better times with her. The country was still struggling to get back on its feet after the war. At the time things still looked bleak. Our troops were fighting in Korea. There was growing civil unrest in Kenya. Before the year was out Britain would test its first atom bomb. The people had hope for a brighter future, but worried in case the second half of the century was no better than the first.

Bottom: The celebrations in Finchley for Queen Elizabeth's coronation began in earnest on 30 May 1953, several days before the real event. They continued until 13 June. Not for these people one day of fun. They made a fortnight of it. Well, why not? It was going to be a long time before another coronation would come along. The monarch was only 27 when she was crowned. Many of her subjects would not live to see her successor take throne, whenever that was going to be. Grand balls, fetes and parties were held in her honour. When the carnival procession rolled through Finchley 20,000 packed the streets to enjoy the day. Lorries were pressganged into being floats. Tableaux of our glorious past were staged on

the backs of vehicles that normally carried coal, vegetables or building materials. They were festooned in Union flags and banners. Floral displays and ribbons turned motorised workhorses into moving pageants. Red, white and blue was everywhere. Coloured triangles of cloth hung on strings from lamp-posts and across the streets. Finchley attracted a number of wealthy Londoners to make their home here in the 18th and 19th centuries. In more recent times show business stars have made there home around Finchley and other parts of the Borough of Barnet. But, whatever their social standing, they all shared the country's joy when the Archbishop of Canterbury, Dr Fisher, heard the Queen take the Coronation Oath.

When Queen Elizabeth II visited the girls' grammar school that bore her name she was making history. On 17 November 1957 she became the first reigning monarch to make an official visit to a state school. Of course it was not named after her as it opened in 1888, close to the Cottage Hospital. It took its name from Elizabeth's Tudor namesake. A new hall and classroom extensions were added in 1938. The Duchess of Kent was asked to perform the opening ceremony in 1938 that also marked the school's half centenary. She was the popular Princess Marina whose husband was killed in a plane crash in 1942. Her niece had only been on the throne for five years when she met Alderman Harold Fern and other members of the council. As befits a woman in high office she kept her gloves firmly in place. The headmistress knew her place. Freda Balaam stood one step behind the Queen as the introductions were made. Miss Balaam organised the girls' education, was responsible for the deployment of the staff and carried the can if anything went wrong. Despite her vast experience and the heavy burden she carried the headmistress played second fiddle to the councillors. Nothing much has changed. Politicians who do not know one end of a piece of chalk from another still make policy and take the credit for success. Guess who gets the brickbats when there is a problem.

High days & holidays

If it was not bad enough to have to sit at a school desk all week then, for some, there were the rigours of Sunday School to undergo. It was not enough to learn your times table during the week and go to church service on Sunday morning. For children of the righteous there was another hour of sitting still to be endured. Imagine the revolt in the ranks of modern youth if they had to do as they were told in this day and age. You cannot even get them to turn up through the school gates from Monday to Friday these days, much less put on their best bib and tucker on a Sunday. Children now expect to be taken out for the day to a theme park or to put on their best replica soccer shirt and go to a match televised by Sky. There was once a time when Sunday was a day of rest. This class of children had been well scrubbed before turning out. Every face shone brightly. Hair was neatly brushed and tortoiseshell hair slides put into place. Overcoats and jackets were the smartest that they owned. Children learned more about the Bible stories they had listened to in school. Their little mouths gaped open as they heard about the whale that swallowed Jonah or the trumpet call that toppled Jericho's walls. Others prepared for their first Communion or took part in Confirmation classes. They recited their catechism before going home for crumpets toasted in front of an open fire.

Left: Every district has its customs and traditions. Some are steeped in the history of the area. Others are concerned with ancient fertility rites. There can even be an element of we have always done it but we don't know why! In rural areas people dance round maypoles and Morrismen spark their clogs. This is a reminder of when country folk circled a living tree as part of their spring rites. Elsewhere there are rushbearing festivals. Many Lancashire and Yorkshire people still hold carnivals during what they call Wakes Weeks, though this history is more recent as it is linked with the old textile industry. Nottingham has its goose fair and Honiton celebrates its lace. Happy marriages are honoured by a flitch and countless village populations roll eggs down the hillside at Easter. All these quaint traditions, festivals and practices have a meaning and interest that marks this country out as something special, if slightly odd to visitors from overseas. Whether or not these lads fully understood what they were doing is not very important. What matters is that they were continuing to practise the ceremony of beating the bounds. As happy as Larry splashing around in the water they had fun with their sticks and poles. Every so often they made sure that where they were beating made the others wet through. The little imps did not get away with it for long. The sterner menfolk watching from above made sure that decorum returned.

Above: The early summer sun was casting its shadows on the Cromer Road schoolchildren as they made their way to morning lessons in May 1954. Their satchels were crammed with pencil cases and homework books. The little girls might stop off for two ounces of jelly babies or a sherbet dip before heading off to the playground. If they had saved enough pocket money a copy of Girls' Crystal or School Friend was waiting for them at the newsagent's. The adventures of the Secret Three, their jolly japes in the school dorm and tales of midnight feasts kept readers happy. These girls were part of the baby boom years. The birth rate soared in the first few years after the war. Men returning from the front did what came naturally and their wives were only too pleased to make up for lost time! The results are seen in the quintet being shepherded across the road by the figure who would never become known as a crossing patrol warden. He was the lollipop man, pure and simple. His job is slightly different today. Half a century ago he stopped passing traffic to let the kiddies cross over. In this millennium he halts the very cars that have brought the children to school. Youngsters now look horrified if they are asked to walk a few hundred yards. Perhaps one day they might rediscover that they can put one foot in front of another.

Above: The League of Health and Beauty put on a special display at Underhill as part of the celebrations for George V's Silver Jubilee. The girls were caught in an unfortunate pose. They looked as if they were giving a Nazi salute. Happily, for once, the camera does lie. The routine had just reached this point in the exercise when the image was frozen for all time. The crowds watching included a number of older people who felt this was yet more evidence of the decadence of youth. Every generation thinks that about the next one. We should remember that it had only been in recent years that mixed bathing was allowed in public swimming pools. Women did not get full voting rights until 1928 and they were anxious to make up for lost time. The newly found freedom gave them greater licence to please themselves in fashion and recreation. Greater involvement in sport and an urge for developing beautiful and healthy bodies helped movements like the League of Health and Beauty flourish. The girls practised hard in local gyms to prove that exercise was fun and fashionable too. The sight of young women clad in vests and showing ample stretches of leg shocked one half of the audience but gave the others a most pleasant experience!

Above right: The playing fields at Underhill were named in honour of King George V, our monarch from 1910 to 1936. The 'Sailor King' was a popular figure with his subjects. During World War I he endeared himself to the troops by making a number of visits to France to see the men at the front. From about 1928 he was in poor health. His people were glad that he survived long enough for them to mark his 25 year reign with joyous celebrations.

This gymnastics' display was put on by the High Barnet Boys' Brigade. They gambolled across the grass like spring lambs. Tumbling routines and handstands made the onlookers marvel at the athletic and skilful way the lads went through their routines. They had been rehearsing for weeks and this was the day when it all came together. Leapfrogging one another and performing somersaults they approached the high spot of their performance. A tricky human pyramid formed, flanked by a circle of other young gymnasts. The applause for their efforts was deafening. If we owned a crystal ball that day the jollity might have been more reserved. In just over four years' time some of the older lads would be practising new drills. They would be learning them on the parade ground under the watchful eye of a sergeant major as they prepared to march off to war. King George did not live to see that day dawn. He died on 20 January 1936. He was sadly missed for his down to earth attitude. He once said, 'I don't like abroad. I've been there.'

Below: Barnet Cinema, also once known as the Cinema Palace, was gutted by fire in 1934. A new building rose from the ashes the following year. The fire created a gap in entertainment for audiences used to at least one visit to the pictures every week. There would be no more Saturday matinées for the youngsters for some time. Courting couples were miffed. They used the back row as a haven of retreat from their frowning parents. A quiet cuddle could be conducted in peace. Usherettes regularly played their torches across the seating just to make sure that the amorous clinches remained modest. Some bespectacled lads turned to their dates, glasses in hand, with the question, 'Do you want to watch the film or ...?' If it was Leslie Howard in 'Of Human Bondage' or Clark Gable's Oscar winning performance in 'It Happened One Night', then he could put his specs back on. The attractions on the silver screen were greater than anything this spotty youth had to offer. He would have to content himself with gazing at Bette Davis or Claudette Colbert. A girl's heart softened as the evening drew on. After being given an ice cream at the interval she allowed her boyfriend to hold her hand during the second half. As he walked her home, stopping off for a fish and chip supper wrapped in an old copy of the Barnet Press, she smiled to herself as an arm encircled her waist.

Bottom: The Barnet reopened as a cinema in 1935. It had been badly damaged by fire the year before. Its new face welcomed cinemagoers who thrilled to the exploits of Errol Flynn, Douglas Fairbanks and Greta Garbo. The Barnet was more than just a cinema. It was a multi faceted entertainment experience. There was a café and dance hall for those who wanted a night out rich in enjoyment. The old cinema had opened on Boxing Day 1912. Short silent movies attracted large audiences. Moustached villains were hissed from the auditorium as they tied winsome heroines to the

railway tracks. How the viewers cheered when the hero cut her free, just as the train thundered into view. Sweeping piano chords and arpeggios accompanied moments of high passion. The stars of those days before talkies included Theda Bara, the vamp whose seductive ways lured men to destruction. While the men adored her sultry charms as Cleopatra or Salome women swooned over Rudolph Valentino. His handsome features in 'The Sheik' and 'The Eagle' caused many a heart to flutter. The 1930s was the golden age of Hollywood. Talking pictures killed off the careers of some silent movie stars whose voices were not suited to the new medium. But a new breed of talent came along to make the pulses race. The Barnet closed in August 1959 and was replaced by a supermarket.

Left: Professional soccer squads boast several dozen players who are listed as potential first teamers. When this photograph was taken Barnet FC could only muster 13. The club was playing in the days when a ten shilling note stuffed in a player's sock was the only sort of financial reward he could hope to get. Now that even second rate players expect wages of over £1 million per year we realise that football is no longer played for entertainment. It is big business. This old team photograph reminds us of how it was. Spectators sit in stadiums segregated from opposition fans. Gone are the days when they stood side by side, exchanging cheery banter and sharing a cup of Bovril. Any use of foul language if a child was nearby was quickly shouted down. On the pitch the centre forward happily shoulder charged the goalkeeper trying to bounce a heavy, sodden lump of leather around the penalty area. It was tough being a centre half, trying to head away a crossed football that had more in common with a cannonball. Barnet FC was founded in 1888. One of its finest hours came at Stamford Bridge in 1946 when the mighty Bishop Auckland was beaten 3-2 in the FA Amateur Cup Final. The club turned professional in 1965. With the irrepressible Barry Fry as manager, promotion to the Football League was won in 1991. Over 5,000 crammed into Underhill Stadium to witness the first ever top-flight match. The opponents played the role of party pooper. Crewe won by the remarkable score of 7-4.

Above: The Star Hotel, 108 High Street, was one of many drinking places that stood on this part of the Great North Road. At one time there were so many pubs, hotels and inns along here that boozers off on a pub crawl did not get very far. If they had a pint in each hostelry the journey up the road could be measured in yards, not furlongs. The families scurrying by the front of the Star in 1934 were passing what had once been the Cock Inn. During its time it had been an alehouse, a coffeehouse and an inn and hotel. In 1872 it boasted five bedrooms and stabling for 28 horses. Coaches regularly called in earlier times for refreshment and a change of team. The Star was remodelled in 1930. In those days it was very much a male bastion, as were most pubs. Unescorted women were not accepted as anything other than out of place until the swinging 60s. In the smoky atmosphere of saloon bars and taprooms men discussed football and politics to their hearts' content. The tables echoed to the rattle of dominoes. Crib boards clattered as matchsticks were used to record pegging scores for card games of don and cribbage. Bets were placed on hands of solo whist and bookies' runners discreetly slipped in and out of the bars, money and slips carefully hidden from the prying eyes of the authorities.

Better buildings by design

We all need somewhere to live. And we are all fascinated with the houses for sale in estate agents windows. How often have we thought 'wouldn't it be nice to live there' when a particular property catches our fancy? But as we all know only too well not all houses are the same - some are dreary, unimaginative buildings of little or no architectural merit whilst others are, in their own way, works of art, a tribute to both the architect who designed them and to the builders who constructed them.

Barnet has its share of every kind of house, but the discerning resident of the area or the visitor from further afield will, if they keep their eyes open, eventually notice that some of the properties built over the last quarter of a century stand out amongst the rest for their exceptional quality of design and workmanship.

The well-known Barnet-based building firm of Oliver & Saunders (Developments) Ltd company can trace its roots back to the firm of J J Oliver Contractors (Barnet) Ltd, a firm founded by a builder, the late John Oliver, in 1975. John Oliver, born in Hornsey in 1941, attended Tottenham Techincal College where he gained his qualifications in plumbing and heating engineering. Aged 21, he established John Oliver Contractors, specialising in shop fitting and refurbishment of commercial properties

throughout London. During the 1970s the firm began to diversify into housing contracts.

At around the same time Paul Saunders, born in North London in 1947, had formed the firm of A B Knight Ltd a company trading as a confirming house for the import and export of goods to and from West Africa. The A B Knight company handled goods as diverse as diesel engines to Lucozade and from electrical accessories to stock fish.

By 1979 Paul Saunders had been successful enough to be able to afford to build his own house. A plot was acquired in Totteridge and Paul Saunders turned to his long time friend John Oliver to build his new home. The time the two spent together on that single house-building project led to the idea of forming Oliver & Saunders Ltd.

Although not officially an Oliver & Saunders (Developments) Ltd project - since that firm had yet to come into being - the first speculative joint venture was funded by A B Knight Ltd and involved the conversion

Above left: Paul Saunders (square picture) and John Oliver. Above right: The company's certificate of incorporation, dated 28th May 1975.
Below: The Snowhill development, St George's Hill.

into two flats of 163, East Barnet Road bought for the grand sum of £19,000.

Oliver & Saunders (Developments) Ltd was launched on the back of this with a share capital of two £1 shares. The new firm's two directors were Paul Saunders and John Oliver whilst the company secretary Mrs Jackie Manaley was seconded from A B Knight. Jackie Manaley holds the position of company secretary to the present day.

At the outset the company's objectives were explicit: strictly starter homes. According to Paul Saunders 'we set out to build starter homes to a level of quality not readily available at that time in what was an

Top: *Glyn Avenue, New Barnet.*
Below: *Lynwood, Totteridge.*

extremely competitive market place'. On 5th March 1982 Oliver & Saunders (Developments) Ltd was registered with the NHBC at 24 Station Road in 400 square feet of office space on loan from A B Knight.

In January 1983 the first official Oliver & Saunders (Developments) Ltd building project was at 88/89 Woodville Road, New Barnet; once the site was acquired work commenced within a month. John Oliver's son, Andrew Oliver, joined the company from building college at this time and six newly built residential flats came to market twelve months later.

During this period Oliver & Saunders relocated to Union Street, High Barnet. This office, part of the larger Gillings Leather Factory Estate was refurbished and was to be Oliver & Saunders (Developments) Ltd's base of operations for next 18 months. The new premises had been purchased by A B Knight Ltd and refurbished by Oliver & Saunders Ltd; at the same time by sub division the main factory was converted into 18 small workshop units continuing to provide work for fledgling building company.

1984 and 85 saw more work for the firm including two office developments at 27 and 29/31 East Barnet Road, now known as Oliver House and Knight House. Two separate residential flat developments at 38 & 40 Potters Road, New Barnet were also completed providing a total of 30 residential flats. In 1985 Andrew Oliver's brother Matthew joined the firm after also studying at college.

Early the following year Oliver & Saunders relocated to the recently completed Knight House whist the acquisition of further sites at Station Road and Lyonsdown Road in New Barnet led to the firm completing an impressive total of 106 residential flats.

1987 saw the commencement of work at 36 Wood Street High Barnet where 31 flats on the Gillings factory estate would be completed. Spring 1987 saw the acquisition of 53 Gloucester Road, New Barnet whilst in June of that year Oliver & Saunders started their biggest project to date at Glyn Avenue, New Barnet where 71 housing units would eventually be completed.

That same period brought investment in the company from the 3iii bank. 3iii bought a 25 per cent share-holding allowing the still young building company to shift financial gear an investment which would result in far more ambitious projects than those tackled to date. 3iii is still involved today with 3iii's Sir James Harvie-Watt the current Chairman of Oliver & Saunders (Developments) Ltd.

An ever increasing architectural load led to architect Don Gallagher being recruited part-time to lighten the load for Oliver & Saunders' full-time architect Steve Coulson. The

Victoria hospital falls into neglect

DISTRICT general manager of Barnet Health Authority Nigel Weaver says there is "an air of neglect falling over Victoria Maternity Hospital."

Sydney Chapman, MP for Chipping Barnet, wrote to the authority about the future of 'The Vic' after an approach by the Barnet Society.

Mr Weaver wrote back saying officers were preparing proposals to develop the site and have employed an architect to advise them.

The hospital was closed at the beginning of 1988 because of lack of staff.

He said: "It is clear that to adapt the existing maternity hospital would be uneconomical. We are having to bear in mind the listing of this building for architectural interest and of course its importance in the conservation area of Wood Street.

"It would be in everybody's interests if we could bring forward a proposal that would actually enhance the building."

Mr Chapman said two things were urgently needed: a new maternity unit at Barnet General Hospital and the renovation and reconstruction of the old cottage hospital.

unexpected departure of Steve Coulson some months later led to Don Gallagher giving up his 'early retired' status to cover full-time; 13 years later he was still the driving force behind the company's production of working drawings!

The year 1988 brought the acquisition of 53 Wood Street, a redundant council-run nursery school. As a Grade II listed building refurbishment as offices was the obvious direction for its future. Listed status and location within a conservation area led to the sympathetic restoration of what, 12 months later, was to become Oliver & Saunders (Developments) Ltd's permanent headquarters. Three months prior to completion of that project, on 10th February 1989, John Oliver suffered a fatal heart attack.

In memory of John Oliver, the newly restored building was named John Oliver Buildings and the firm of Oliver & Saunders (Developments) Ltd took up residence three months later. The tragic loss of one of its two founders led to the hurried recruitment of the current Construction

Both pages: *The Victoria Maternity Hospital, 1939 - 1945, the war years.*

Director David Hampson from one of Oliver & Saunders' competitors, Summit Homes.

At the time of John Oliver's death, 71 units were approaching completion at Glyn Avenue whilst at Park Road, New Barnet, the firm's biggest project to date comprising 106 units the company was six months into the construction programme.

Although purchased in late 1987 work did not commence at Hagden Lane, Watford until October 1990 where 85 units of residential flats would eventually be completed. This marked the start of Oliver & Saunders maturing as a company which was confident and experienced enough to mount building projects outside the immediate Barnet area. That growing confidence coincided with the recession of the late 1980s and early 1990s which damaged many similar firms. Fortunately the Watford site had been acquired at a favourable price and that, together with excellent planning results, meant that the project was highly successful at a time when many larger companies were undergoing major financial problems.

The year 1990 also saw the purchase of land for 46 houses and flats at Colney Hatch Lane, Friern Barnet and at The Ridgeway, Cuffley in Hertfordshire. Oliver & Saunders (Developments) Ltd's first venture up the residential market since the home John Oliver built for Paul Saunders

was at Cuffley. The Ridgeway was a large detached house built on a one acre plot on the best road in the area and sold for around £600,000. A luxury field which the company was to return to some years later.

Also in 1990 was the purchase of St Cross Chambers in Upper Marsh Lane Hoddesdon which led to a seven thousand square feet office refurbishment project.

In March 1991 the purchase of land on Bushey Hall Road Watford for 132 units of mixed flats and houses led to the end of Oliver & Saunders (Developments) Ltd as primarily a builder of starter homes.

The decision to lead the company up market began with the purchase of the Victoria Maternity Hospital immediately adjacent to John Oliver Buildings and at the time falling quietly into disrepair.

The house, originally known as Cedar Lawn, was acquired by the firm in 1991; it had been built in 1766 and this Grade II listed building was once been the home of William Cattley (1788-1835) a famous botanist and the first successful grower of epiphytic orchids in Britain. In 1888 the property changed use with the founding of the cottage hospital. Substantially enlarged in 1898 the building was transferred in 1923 to the Barnets as the Victoria Hospital, later specialising as the area's maternity hospital.

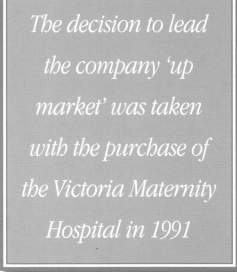

The decision to lead the company 'up market' was taken with the purchase of the Victoria Maternity Hospital in 1991

The hospital was closed in 1987 as surplus to requirements by the local heath authority. The building was empty for some time and fell into disrepair. After being acquired in March 1991 by Oliver & Saunders a further three years of planning negotiation began. Work on restoration and building new elements on the site commenced in 1994. After two years work, 21 prestigious residential units were able to be offered for sale.

The long term negotiations with the planning authorities and English Heritage had led to a period of five years between the purchase and completion of the Victoria project, the elapse of time was something which earlier developers clearly had in mind: - a time capsule was found during refurbishment containing newspapers and journals from 1823 when Evelyne Baldwin had laid a commemorative stone after the hand-over to the Barnets. All the material found was re-interred along with new material upon completion of the restoration in 1996.

Meanwhile Oliver & Saunders (Developments) Ltd had purchased a site for four houses at Beech Hill, Hadley Wood in September 1993. Five bedrooms, three receptions and price tag just short of a cool, half a million pounds was the specification. All four were snapped up by local buyers as each reached completion. The writing was on the wall - and the development was quickly followed by a similar one at Tanglewood, Rockways Arkley.

In May 1994 land was acquired for two houses in Milespit Hill, Mill Hill. 50 per cent bigger than Hadley Wood these properties sold from plan; also five bedroom houses these 3,400 square foot homes included features for which Oliver & Saunders was soon to become well known: en suite bathrooms, utility rooms, family rooms and the inclusion of an already converted attic space to provide a sixth bedroom or playroom.

Above: *Union Street.*
Below: *John Oliver Buildings.*

businesses have grown with it and now find themselves too trading in areas previously unknown to them.

The year 1996 saw work commence on two houses on Barnet Road, Arkley, a site which had been partly developed three years earlier as Tanglewood. The long term resident of the existing house was keen to acquire one of the new Oliver & Saunders properties just completed at Cattley Close as the Victoria hospital site is known today.

In 1989 Paul Saunders and John Oliver had made the decision to buy a parcel of land in Cuffley which proved that even the most experienced sometimes get it wrong. For the previous twenty-eight years the land had been subject to onerous planning conditions and uncooperative parties on all sides. In 1996 what had appeared to be an expensive mistake was however transformed into a lucrative project, the final jigsaw piece falling into place. The result was four exceptional houses behind a gated entrance at the top of a three hundred foot private driveway.

1996 continued apace with projects commencing on a large individual property in Beech Hill Avenue, Hadley Wood, another in Denleigh Gardens, Winchmore Hill, three houses in Watford Road, Radlett and yet another three in Hamilton Way, West Finchley. Although each comfortably cost in excess of half a million pounds, and in one case approaching one million, it was not until 1998 that Oliver & Saunders (Developments) Ltd again broke the million pound barrier.

Above left: *Foxlands, Totteridge.*
Top: *Hornbeams, Totteridge.*

The Mill Hill development was soon followed by three more luxury houses at Lynford Lodge, Arkley. Foxlands in Totteridge Lane was acquired in late 1994 and the house erected there at 5,200 square feet built from handmade bricks was not only the firm's largest home to date but also the first to exceed a million pounds sale price when it was sold in 1996. Nine months after Foxlands was purchased, Hornbeams, the adjacent plot was purchased and the two projects ran simultaneously side by side. Again neither property was to see the light of an estate agent's window both being sold almost immediately by local agents Blades in Totteridge and Statons in High Barnet.

As a company based in and building in and around Barnet, Oliver & Saunders (Developments) Ltd has traditionally drawn most of its work force from the locality, from directly employed staff to sub contractors supplying plumbing services down to printers supplying stationery. As the company has grown and diversified, many local

Purchased in 1995 Lynwood in Totteridge proved to be a new phase in the company's ambitions. With its conception as a stand alone property in the very best location and a review of specification of both design and materials the property went to market in 1998 with the banner flying. Stand alone properties with staff and games quarters became features of the company product, oak feature staircases and internal doors, polished granite kitchen work-surfaces, were all set behind electronically operated entrance gates. The one million pound barrier was a thing of the past.

Oliver & Saunders (Developments) Ltd was now firmly in the luxury house bracket of building developers. That status was empha-sised with the commencement of two projects on Camlet Way, Hadley Wood - the Rowans and Oakdene as the houses were known which reinforced all the values now perceived as attributes of buying an Oliver and Saunders home.

Whilst public attention was being focused towards completed projects, the company land team quietly bought up ever more impressive sites for the architects, still under the careful guidance of David Hampson, to work on during 1997. The Dutch Cottage and Hadar both in Totteridge, three more magnificent houses, were soon to be added to

the company's portfolio. As work commenced in mid 1998 it was clear that Oliver & Saunders (Developments) Ltd was ready to move into new territory.

Surrey's property 'Golden Triangle' was selected - the district between Cobham, Esher and Weybridge is an area of large private estates and luxury homes. The most presti-gious of them all is the St George's Hill estate: 900 acres of private land, 24 hour security controlled access, two international golf courses and approxi-mately 400 individual homes at prices of between one and five million pounds.

Snowhill, purchased in September 1998, was a one acre, south-facing plot, located in the heart of this prestigious estate. Two months later 11 acres of prime Surrey woodland were bought as a site for two new homes. Silverwood was a derelict house set in a three acre clearing within that woodland.

In 1999 as construction got underway in Surrey, the Dutch Cottage in Totteridge was nearing completion and by mid summer, just weeks after its completion, the property was purchased by an overseas client for 2.5 million pounds.

This page: *Park Road, Appletree Gardens.*

Nearby Hadar was now mid way through construction being acclaimed Best Luxury/Select Development in Site magazine's Site of the Year Awards.

In the same year the company's site manager, Len Jones, won the prestigious NHBC 'Pride in the Job Award' for his management skills over several of Oliver & Saunders recent projects.

By March 2000 Hadar went to market with two homes in Totteridge in excess of 6,000 square feet and an asking prices of over two million pounds each. Snowhill in Surrey sold within four hours of its launch for £2.25 million. Surrey is off to a great start, Silverwood Plot One sold for £2.75 million during construction.

With future projects underway both in Surrey and the home territory the company moves into the new millennium confident of maintaining its position as Barnet's premier house builder in the decades to come.

History and the creation of 'heritage' are ongoing processes. Many, perhaps most of the properties built during the latter half of the twentieth century will not outlast the lives of the younger members of our community, their shelf life being less than our own average lifespan. Some buildings, such as those of Oliver & Saunders however, are built to such a high standard that they are cherished in a way that the plain brick and concrete boxes that have been so much a feature of the English house building scene since the 1940s will never be. Oliver & Saunders has in reality been helping build Barnet's history as well as building houses.

Top: *Dutch Cottage, Totteridge.*
Below (both pictures): *Hadar, Totteridge.*

Numbed residents pick through the debris of Oakmere House, Bells Hill, Chipping Barnet. The scene was repeated night after night in the capital and its suburbs during those months that came to be known as the Blitz. During the late summer of 1940 Goering's Luftwaffe had sent wave after wave of fighters and bombers across the Channel. The plan was to knock out Britain's air defences by destroying airfields and the planes of the RAF. Then the invasion of England would be a simple matter for the German armed forces. What became known as the Battle of Britain was fought out in the skies over the south and east coasts. Our brave boys, backed by superb support on the ground, won the day. In a vengeful counter strike the enemy leader, Adolf Hitler, ordered the aerial assault on British cities. The civilian population was the target. Hitler hoped to bomb us into submission. From September onwards London suffered nine months of moonlight bombing. Hull, Liverpool, Coventry, Glasgow and so many other cities were targeted, but the capital took the brunt. Of 92,000 civilians killed a quarter were Londoners. On 6 November 1940 a parachute mine fell on Oakmere, an old people's home. Containing a ton of explosive it killed 17 people and injured 31, including some nurses. The borough of Barnet lost 402 of its community in the first two months of the onslaught. Although the British resolve to resist was stiffened, there is no denying the sheer terror felt by those who heard the whine of the bombs as they fell to earth close by.

The People's War

Battered but unbowed, damaged but not broken. That was the spirit that got Londoners through the war. This was just one of countless scenes of bomb damage inflicted upon our city in 1941. It had been going on since September 1940. Wave after wave of Heinkels, Dorniers and Junkers brought their nightly cargoes of death and destruction. Searchlights panned the skies and ack-ack tracer shells chased the bombers who came to try to hammer us into submission. Our Spitfires and Hurricanes did their best to throw back each attack, but they came in such huge numbers. It was inevitable that many got through to deposit their loads on industry and innocent citizens alike. It became a regular event to take to the Underground stations for safety. Others went to the Anderson shelters to wait for the all clear to sound. All the while people were there they listened to the rumbling and crashes outside. When it was safe to come out they did so with fear in their hearts. Picking their way through smouldering embers of fire ravaged streets and highways strewn with rubble they steeled themselves for what they would find at home. Would they still have a home to go to or had it become just another statistic? On one night in May 1941 a force of 550 planes dropped hundreds of high explosive bombs and 100,000 incendiaries on London, killing 1,400. Fortunately, the enemy turned its attention to invading Russia that summer. We were spared further onslaughts for three years. Then it was the turn of the V1 and V2 rockets to create mayhem.

Both pages: In 1939 Britain's Prime Minister Neville Chamberlain had made his announcement to the waiting people of Britain that '...this country is at war with Germany.' The country rolled up its sleeves and prepared for the inevitable. This war would be different from other wars. This time planes had the ability to fly further and carry a heavier load, and air raids were fully expected. Air raid shelters were obviously going to be needed, and shelters were built in areas such as the sandstone cliffs bordering Chestergate.

By the time war was declared an army of volunteers of both sexes had already been recruited to form an Air Raid Protection service. At first ARP personnel were unpaid volunteers but when war broke out in

September 1939 they became paid staff. It was their job to patrol specified areas, making sure that no chinks of light broke the blackout restrictions, checking the safety of local residents, being alert for gas attacks, air raids and unexploded bombs. The exceptional work done by Air Raid Wardens in dealing with incendiaries, giving first aid to the injured, helping to rescue victims from their bombed-out properties, clearing away rubble, and a thousand and one other tasks became legendary; during the second world war nearly as many private citizens were killed as troops - and many of them were the gallant ARP wardens.

At the beginning of the war Sir Anthony Eden, Secretary of State for War, appealed in a radio broadcast for men between 17 and 65 to make up a new force, the Local

Defence Volunteers, to guard vulnerable points from possible Nazi attack. Within a very short time the first men were putting their names down. At first the new force had to improvise: there were no weapons to spare and men had to rely on sticks, shotguns handed in by local people, and on sheer determination. Weapons and uniforms did not become available for several months.

In July the Local Defence Volunteers was renamed the Home Guard, and by the following year were a force to be reckoned with. Television programmes such as 'Dad's Army' have unfortunately associated the Home Guard with comedy, but in fact they performed much important work. The Guard posted sentries to watch for possible aircraft or parachute landings at likely spots such as disused aerodromes, golf courses on the outskirts of towns, local parks and racecourses. They manned anti-aircraft rocket guns, liaised with other units and with regular troops, set up communications and organised balloon barrages.

Other preparations were hastily made. Place names and other identifying marks were obliterated to confuse the enemy about exactly where they were. Notices went up everywhere giving good advice to citizens on a number of issues. 'Keep Mum - she's not so dumb' warned people to take care what kind of information they passed on, as the person they were speaking to could be an enemy.

Older people will remember how difficult it was to find certain items in the shops during the war; combs, soap, cosmetics, hairgrips, elastic, buttons, zips - all were virtually impossible to buy as factories that once produced these items had been turned over to war work. Stockings were in short supply, and resourceful women resorted to colouring their legs with gravy browning or with a mixture of sand and water. Beetroot juice was found to be a good substitute for lipstick.

Clothes rationing was introduced in 1941, and everyone had 66 coupons per year. Eleven coupons would buy a dress, and sixteen were needed for a coat. The number of coupons was later reduced to 40 per person. People were required to save material where they could - ladies' hemlines went up considerably, and skirts were not allowed to have lots of pleats. Some found clever ways around the regulations by using materials that were not rationed. Blackout material could be embroidered and made into blouses or skirts, and dyed sugar sacks were turned into curtains.

Left: Hendon Show had been a regular occasion to display agricultural expertise. During the week of 31 July-7 August 1943 it took on a new significance. The advertising board outside the library posed an important question and supplied the two answers. Moving food supplies around the country was a drain on the transport resources. Precious petrol and diesel was needed elsewhere. Lorries were required to transport troops, supplies and equipment for the armed forces. The railway wagons needed to take similar cargoes, as well as coal, iron and oil to the industries essential to the war effort. National food stocks were, in any case, running low. We could not rely on imports from our allies. So much of our merchant navy had been lost in attacks upon its convoys. During the previous year a monthly total of 650,000 tons of Allied shipping had gone to the bottom of the ocean. Wolf packs of U-boats, under the command of Admiral Karl Doenitz, called the shots. The threat only receded with better technology in developing a new radar system and better Asdic detection sets later in the war. In 1943 rationing of even basic foodstuffs was biting hard. 'Dig for victory' became a national slogan. Every spare piece of land was dug over and planted out. Back gardens grew cabbages. Playing fields became huge allotments. Even roadside verges were cultivated. The Food Minister, Lord Woolton, recommended a new cookery book, 'A Kitchen Goes to War', advising housewives on recipes to be concocted from the meagre rations. One dish, a mixture of turnips, carrots, parsnips and other vegetables, was christened 'Woolton Pie'. It was revolting.

Above: This is not a wartime picture as you might think. It dates from 1954. Even though we were not officially at war with anyone there was still a need for members of civil defence organisations to be on their toes. This was an early period in the long cold war that existed between the free world and communism. Winston Churchill spoke of an iron curtain being drawn across Europe. Spies were thought to be everywhere. Senator McCarthy led the 'reds under the bed' witch hunt to rid America of communist sympathisers. At home Kim Philby was investigated as the 'third man' behind the earlier defection to Russia of the two British agents Burgess and MacLean. The testing of atomic bombs and the threat of nuclear war meant that Britain was staying alert for any threat from the eastern bloc that would come together in the Warsaw Pact the following year. The civil defence manoeuvres took place at Church Farm, East Barnet, near the church of St Mary the Virgin. The farmhouse dated from c 1660 and 200 years later a Boys' Farm Home was established there. Its intended use was to provide accommodation and work for poor orphans. From the age of six children cultivated the farm's 50 acres. Voluntary contributions and Home Office grants kept the Farm Home going. It came under council control in 1938 and was demolished in the 1960s. The civil defence volunteers practised survival techniques and rescue procedures on the land once tilled by children who might have drifted into crime until rescued by the courts from failing families.

Below centre: Boots Pharmacy has been remodelled, but still keeps the same site today as it did in 1933. Most Boots' stores originally had specially named departments. They included chemistry, toilet, library and fancy goods. This shop was one of the chain founded by Jesse Boot of Nottingham. He saw his stores develop from the humble chemist shop, with its simple range of medicines, to an institution on every high street. A range of perfumes, toiletries and beauty aids was added. It could have been called the 'sweet smell of success'. He became well loved for his charity work. His efforts were rewarded when he became Lord Trent. He died in 1931. Boots became a favourite shopping place for youngsters to find a birthday present for mum or gran. No anniversary was complete without a gift of bath salts or talcum powder. Sometimes dad received a bottle of aftershave. Whether he liked it or not he had to wince as he splashed the stuff onto his freshly shaved face. He did not want to disappoint the kids, even if it did bring tears to his eyes. The bank has since changed hands, but the building still carries out similar business. It is now occupied by HSBC. The jeweller's to the right of the new Woolworth's site is now a toy shop. Woolworth's came and went. The Abbey National building now fills the space.

Bottom: The mayor cut a proud figure in his ceremonial robes. He was standing in front of Hendon Town Hall receiving the salute of the troops passing by. Tanks and armoured vehicles trundled along the road. The whole country was rocking. On 11 May 1941 London suffered its heaviest single night's raid of the Blitz. The mayors of Westminster and Bermondsey were among the 1,400 civilians who were killed. In the European theatre British troops were overrun in Greece. It was one of the grimmest periods of the war. A week after the massive air raid saw the start of War Weapons Week. During 17-24 May people were encouraged to make a special push for the war effort. With U-boats prowling the seas the country was unable to bring in enough raw materials to meet the demands of the armed forces for more tanks, planes, battleships and ammunition. Every householder was urged to turn his thoughts to donating whatever he could for salvage. Anything that could be melted down and recycled was acceptable. Communities were involved in competitions to see which ones could top the league table for donations. Thermometers charting their progress appeared on the front of public buildings. It is ironic that a later plane was nicknamed the 'Flying Bedstead'. The newly built wartime Spitfire might originally have been just that.

Street scenes

Eric J Wills hung out of the upstairs window of AJ Wills & Co grocer's shop to capture Barnet High Street as it looked in 1935. The buildings next door to Jenkins now reflect that finance is the cornerstone of modern life. These days they belong to Nationwide and Lloyds TSB. The Salisbury Hotel sign no longer hangs outside 126 High Street. It can be seen in the local museum. The hotel closed in 1986, being demolished two years later. A supermarket has since been built on the site. The original Salisbury opened for business as the Tabard on the Hoope. Further name changes saw it become the Tabor and Pipe and then the Royal Waggon. It had been built in a Georgian style, flush with the pavement. There were stables to the rear and the hotel included an auction room that doubled on occasions as a concert room. In more modern times dinner dances were frequently held as clubs and societies hosted regular functions there. The Salisbury owes its final name change to the opportunism of the Royal Waggon landlord in 1821. Competition between the many coaching inns was keen. An agreement was struck with Lord Salisbury to supply him with post horses at a cheaper rate than that offered by rival inns. In return he granted the pub the right to use his name. It was a famous name. The first Earl of Salisbury was Robert Cecil, chief minister to Queen Elizabeth I. Robert Gascoyne-Cecil, the third marquis and Earl of Salisbury, became prime minister on three separate occasions in the latter years of Queen Victoria's reign. The old Salisbury was rebuilt in 1927.

Above: The 1935 view, taken from the window of 128 High Street, shows a busy Barnet. Even before the second world war the motor car was threatening to clog the road through the town centre. This section of the street runs almost from the junction with St Albans Road along to the old Wesleyan church that is now home to the Spires shopping centre. The entrance to the galleria and attractively paved courtyards, with their benches and pretty shrubs, has kept the turrets of the old church. It was demolished in 1989. Wesley Hall, a new Methodist church, stands behind the centre on Stapylton Street. It also has a similar roof styling. It was the 18th century Anglican clergyman, John Wesley, who helped found the Methodist movement within the Church of England. The Methodists had a tightly knit system of church government. It combined a strong central authority with effective local organisation. The employment of lay preachers enabled the movement to expand rapidly throughout the 19th century. Methodism was especially successful in the expanding industrial areas, where it helped the working people to overcome economic depression by spiritual means. The movement aimed to help people raise their economic status as well, by encouraging thrift and simple living. What Wesley would have made of the Kentucky Fried Chicken house that now stands in the distance, who can tell?

Right: To be a photographer you have to have an eye for detail and a flair for appreciating angles and subjects. There are times when you also need nerves of steel and a head for heights. On 6 May 1935 the camera was being pointed from the dizzy heights of the parish church tower, looking north along Barnet High Street. Far away in the distance is the Corn Exchange. It was originally the posting house for the Green Man and was rebuilt as Exchange Buildings in 1890-91. The street from there to the church has always been a busy thoroughfare. A century before this scene was recorded the road echoed to the sound of the horns blown by coachmen warning of the arrival of the mail coach. The horses' hooves and the metal rimmed wheels fairly crashed and rattled on their way to and from the city. The London-Glasgow mail coach would be only a short time into its 42 hour journey when it passed through here. It had come up the roadway of Barnet Hill, built by the Turnpike Trust. By the time Queen Victoria came to the throne 90 coaches a day were passing through the Whetstone turnpike. Although the railway removed the horse drawn long distance coaches from our roads, there were the motor cars to come. In 1922 some 1,500 cars used this road every day. By the end of the decade that figure had risen to 5,000. In addition there were almost as many lorries, motorbikes, buses and pushbikes.

The aerial view of Chipping Barnet was taken in 1955. The bus has just turned from Wood Street to enter High Street. Barnet, or La Barnette as it once was called, probably owes its name to the Anglo Saxon word 'baernet', a place cleared by burning. The whole district was formerly heavily forested. Early settlers would have had to clear a space by torching the trees. Development was slow. The surrounding areas were no more than a series of little hamlets and outlying farms for many centuries. St John the Baptist, that became the parish church in 1866, holds centre stage where the two roads meet. The church was the focal point for the settlement that grew up around it in medieval times, although the first religious building in the area was at East Barnet. St John the Baptist stood largely untouched from the 14th century until 1875. One of the top architects of the Victorian age, William Butterfield, conducted its restoration. He removed the old tower and built a new and higher nave. It was during these days that Barnet saw real growth. From a figure of 8,000 in 1801 the population had grown to 76,000 by the time the 19th century drew to a close. The coming of the age of steam had made the difference. From 1872 the Great Northern Railway opened up new horizons. Commuting to the city became a simple reality. Farmers, merchants and industrialists could move their goods speedily and efficiently.

Above: Riding some buses or trams in the 1930s could be a draughty experience. In bright, sunny weather it was enjoyable to sit on the top deck and indulge in a spot of motorised sunbathing. It was a different story when the wind was blowing and the rain lashing down. The earliest ones had a form of modesty screen to protect women from ogling glances aimed at those brave enough to clamber up the stairway to the top deck. The motorbike and sidecar, passing Hudson's van, was heading towards the White Horse pub and Dolcis Shoe Company building on the right. The ground floor of the 1891 Corn Exchange, on the junction of St Albans Road and High Street, was occupied by Williams Brothers hardware store in the early 1930s. A printing and communications company is in residence today. Motorbikes and sidecars were popular forms of transport through to the 1950s and early 1960s. They were not the safest forms of conveyance, nor were they particularly comfortable. The passengers were vulnerable in any road accident. The two men outside the shop belonging to A Nunnerley & Son, draper and clothier, look very dapper in their fashionable togs. The chap in the plus fours, with his inevitable walking stick, reminds us that Barnet had more links with its rural past than with Greater London in between the wars. His pal was properly dressed in a three piece suit. You did not go to town scruffily or casually dressed in those days.

Above right: When the railway came to Barnet the first station was sited in what became New Barnet. At first it was located in the middle of open countryside, over a mile from the town centre. The earliest passengers had to traipse there to connect with the new form of transport that was the wonder of the age. Station Road was built to help make for easier access to the railway. Horse drawn carriages and buses brought passengers to the station. Others settled in the new housing close by the line and New Barnet rapidly grew into a little town in its own right. The war memorial to the right was erected in 1922. The photograph was taken not long after it had been dedicated. Barclays Bank occupied the left hand end of the building in the centre of the picture. It stayed at 36 Station Road until 1995. It used to display a letter written in 1886 to its directors, asking them to set up a bank in New Barnet. Edward Fergusson Taylor was one of the letter's authors. His estate agency had offices in the right hand end of the same building you are looking at. Fergusson Taylor, as his agency was known, was himself something of a wheeler-dealer. His drive and eye for opportunity did much to help New Barnet's progress in late Victorian times.

THE BOROUGH OF BARNET *Memories*

Below: The aerial view of New Barnet clearly shows the Triangle at the centre of the picture. The church has since been replaced by an office block. New Barnet owes much of its existence to the railway. As train services from Euston to Birmingham became established in the 1840s, traffic on the roads fell away. Stagecoaches were coming to the end of their era. Great Northern Railway (GNR) opened a station here on the Kings Cross to Hitchin line in 1850. People from Chipping Barnet and High Barnet had to make the trek to reach Barnet Station, as it was then called. It was only renamed New Barnet in 1872, when High Barnet got its own station. During the 1850s any land not used by GNR around its first station in the area was developed for roads and housing. The village of New Barnet was brought to life. A thriving Victorian community grew around the spot once known as Lyonsdown. Nearby East Barnet was a district of country estates and splendid mansions. The development of New Barnet, catering for the new breed of commuters using the railway, changed the face of this part of the borough for evermore. The photograph is one of the earliest aerial shots, being taken just before World War I. The railway line at the top of the picture had cut a swathe through the countryside between here and Cockfosters to the east.

Bottom: Hanging on for grim death the photographer pointed his lens south down High Street. The NatWest Bank on the corner of Park Road was built in 1892 as the London County and Westminster Bank. In 1935 the tracks of the electric tramway had only a few short years of life left in them. Cars and tram carriages drove side by side on this wide stretch of road. They developed together, but we all know which one won the race for survival. Trams are making a comeback in some northern cites, like Sheffield, Newcastle, Leeds and Manchester. It is unlikely that Barnet will see them return. There is little space on our streets to support them unless the motor car is completely removed from the main roads into the borough's towns. London saw its first electric trams run along Edgware Road in 1904, providing a link with Cricklewood. The lines reached out from Highgate to Whetstone the following year. By 1907 Barnet residents were able to board their own trams and commute to the city. Greater access to the heart of the capital helped fire an explosion in the borough's population. The 1901 census recorded 76,000 in residence. By 1921 this had doubled. By the time World War II began it had increased by the same factor again to 296,000. In the last 60 years there has been little change in that number. That is no surprise. Where would you put any more?

At the start of the 20th century rows of gas lamps lit up Barnet High Street. It was a road full of small family businesses and numerous pubs. Three of them even stood side by side. The Green Man, Duke of Wellington and The Green Dragon vied for custom near the junction with St Albans Road. As we look towards there in the 1930s, with the Corn Exchange in the distance, the row of cars acts as a reminder that Barnet had developed from the rough and ready place it once had been. An affluence had come and with it the trappings of wealth. Shiny chrome and glistening coachwork belonged to people who had risen above the darkest days of the depression. Whilst many in other parts of the country struggled to

keep house and home together Barnet businessmen more than made ends meet. Commerce had helped create prosperity for the many London tradesmen who lived here in the 17th and 18th centuries. They mainly settled in fine Georgian houses around Hadley Green. In those days the High Street was a wild place to be. As coaches rattled by along the Great North Road waggoners and drovers used to provide a tough clientele in the countless alehouses. Daniel Defoe set one of his adventures of the scurrilous Moll Flanders, the heroine of his 1722 novel, in Barnet. Gradually the influence of the more genteel spread along the road from Hadley. Businesses became more respectable and the area an attractive place to set up shop.

Bottom: Vivian Way, in the early 1960s, was lined with parked cars as Hendon shoppers busied themselves on the pavements that seem a far cry from its historical roots. If you stay close to the town centre Hendon appears to be a place of numerous retail centres. Hendon Central, Brent Street, Ballards Lane and Tally Ho Corner all give the impression that the world is a material one. Thousands of cars are accommodated in Brent Cross Shopping Centre car park and link roads take motorists into the city centre or out to the M1 and M25 motorways. Move away from the centre and there is still something of old Hendon to be found. The parish church and 17th century Church House Farm, on Greyhound Hill, as well as the historic buildings on Church Road provide a flavour of life as it was. Hendon was once a refuge for city dwellers. During the Black Death of the mid 1300s this rural village attracted people escaping from the disease ridden streets of the capital. Famous outsiders have come to live around Hendon in more recent times. One of the first was the actor-manager David Garrick. In the 18th century he settled as Lord of the Manor at Hendon Hall. He placed numerous statues in the grounds that reflected his Shakespearean interests. Nowadays stars of stage, screen and the pop world have taken up residence in the area.

Right: The open air market in full swing on Market Place, alongside Bath Place, was known by several names. They included Mary Payne's Place and the Poor Man's Market. Fruit, vegetables and flowers were on sale in the stalls during the first part of the 20th century. Produce was grown locally and brought into Barnet on carts to be sold on to residents who paid for their purchases with pennies, halfpennies and farthings. This was one of a number of markets dotted around the district. The first one came to Barnet in 1199 when King John granted a charter permitting it to hold a weekly market. The lord of the manor had to pay the king for this right. In return he could control the profits. The original market was established near the parish church. These days it can be found on St Albans Road. Mary Payne's Place only held sway for less than 30 years. Situated opposite the junction of High Street with St Albans Road it swung into action every Wednesday. For the rest of the week it was an open space. Noisy election meetings and other public gatherings were held, some of which got out of hand. The site was always subject to some form of controversy. The Council claimed that the space was part of the highway. A number of stallholders were thrown out. However, the courts ruled that Mary Payne's Place was public land. The victory was short-lived as developers moved in and built on the site.

On the move

Hendon Air Show attracted thousands to the airfield in 1937. It was Coronation year and that seemed to add to the pageantry and sense of occasion. The new king and his family took their places among a crowd estimated at 200,000. The little princesses, Elizabeth and Margaret, were just as thrilled as any other children when 600 planes put on the biggest display ever witnessed. As the day's entertainment began a huge formation of 250 aircraft flew across the area where the royals were sitting. Harrows, Gauntlets and Gladiators blotted out the sun momentarily. The audience oohed and aahed and youngsters clamped their hands over their ears at the deafening fly past. Other spectators viewed from further away. They were still in their cars trying to get to the car parks and fields surrounding Hendon aerodrome. The roads and lanes were clogged as 25,000 vehicles eventually made it to witness the exciting aerobatics and death defying stunts of individual pilots and those flying formation. Simulated dogfights reminded the crowd that one day soon all this technique would be put to the acid test. Old planes from World War I and observation balloons from that era demonstrated how far technology had come in little more than 30 years since the Wright brothers had first left the ground. Significant in the display was the number of single winged bomber planes on show. It would not be long before those watching in 1937 would recognise the sight and sound of German bombers as readily as they spotted the British planes above them on that day.

Above: The first Auxiliary Air Force Squadrons were created in 1925. Hendon Air Station was home to 600 Squadron from January 1927, when it made the short move from Northolt to here. By the summer 601 Squadron was also based at Hendon. The formation of 604 Squadron in 1930 increased the station's importance in Britain's air defences. During the 1930s the country became increasingly restless as Fascism spread across Europe. Hitler became Chancellor of Germany in 1933 and encouraged the dictator, Mussolini, in his flouting of the League of Nation's warnings when Italian forces invaded Abyssinia in 1935. When, the following year, Franco seized power in Spain, prompting three years of civil war, the writing was on the wall. The world was about to return to the battlefield. Aeroplanes would form the front line of any battle. By January 1938 Fighter Command was in the process of forming 26 squadrons. The biplane on camera was a Hawker Demon, belonging to 604 Squadron. A large two seater fighter, it was later succeeded by the Bristol. During 1938 training was stepped up. Air force chiefs placed more faith in the ability of their pilots and the skill of their aircraft designers than they did in the little piece of paper Mr Chamberlain was to bring back from Munich that September. One exercise saw 945 planes take to the air and the Demon played the part of a fighter defending against a bomber raid. The Demons and the rest of 604 Squadron moved to North Weald during this period.

Right: No description of an aerodrome would be complete without an aerial photograph. The Luftwaffe had a similar view when it attacked on a number of occasions during 1940 and at later stages of the war. Hendon did not suffer as badly as some, but it was bad enough. Hangars and neighbouring houses were damaged and destroyed by fire. However, V1 rockets caused more havoc in 1944. Four WAAFs were killed by a flying bomb and, in another assault, all the occupants of a barrack block were wiped out. Hendon's connections with flying had begun in the 1860s when two balloonists made an unscheduled landing there. The true link goes back to 1908. HP Martin and GH Handasyde built a monoplane in the function room at Hendon's Old Welsh Harp pub. It failed its early tests, but EJ Everett was more successful. Not far from the pub Everett was building his first plane in an old garden shed on the edge of what was to become Hendon Aviation Ground. One of his assistants was CR Fairey. He went on to found his own company and produce such aircraft as the Fairey Fox, a two seater light bomber. All this time Claude Grahame-White was developing his interest in anything mechanical. In 1909 he bought an aeroplane from Louis Blériot, the cross Channel flier. Two years later he bought the airfield and put on the first military flying display. He had already established an aviation company and his factory went into increased production during World War I. Three pilots who trained at Hendon at this time went on to win the Victoria Cross.

Below centre: Each Spitfire cost about £6,000 to produce during the war. It was one of the fastest and most effective single seat fighters of World War II. This type of low wing monoplane was highly effective as a defensive interceptor during the Battle of Britain. The Hendon Griffin was one of four built with monies raised through the Hendon Fighter Fund. The smiling pilot was about take part in a sortie in 1942.

The Germans had begun their 'Baedeker' raids on our heritage towns and cities. Coventry, Bath, Exeter, York and Norwich all felt the weight of the bombs that had previously been reserved for the capital and the northern industries and shipyards. Young men who risked their lives in our defence fought the battle for supremacy in the skies. The Hendon Griffin was in operational service from July 1941 to May 1942. It had been dedicated to the 120th Hendon Squadron of the Air Training Corps. Locals were immensely proud that they had been able to raise sufficient funds to get four Spitfires airborne. They had collected cash, recycled books and clothing, run whist drives and white elephant stalls, badgered relatives and donated jewellery to the war effort. Their sacrifices and hard work could be seen flying overhead. The first Spitfire, designed by RJ Mitchell, had flown in 1936. The RAF put it into service in 1938. After the war they continued in active service as reconnaissance planes until 1954.

Bottom: At first there was some opposition to the railway coming to Barnet. In the first wave of track building the steep hill from London to Potters Bar did not encourage engineers to head our way. But locals had their way. It was costly to move goods around on the roads. Farmers were keen to explore the new mode of transport. Commuters were anxious to find a quicker journey to and from their offices in the city. Eventually, GNR opened a station on level ground, some 2 km from the old town, in August 1850. But, don't we just love a good disaster? The little lads watched the scene on 7 August 1953 at High Barnet where a train had overshot the shunting spur of the railway line. Sleepers had been used to stop it falling further down the embankment and onto the Great North Road. The boys probably wished it would do. That would add to the excitement. When they grew up they would enjoy rubber necking on the motorway at road smashes. It must be something in our makeup that causes us to stare at others in trouble. The boys were dressed in the fashion of the middle of the 20th century. Children wore clothing suited to their years. The word 'teenager' was only just being invented and 'tweenies' meant something to do with maids in country houses, not an age group that firms could target. When did you last see a lad in short trousers? In those days they were compulsory wear in primary schools.

supply. Wires danced as the buses approached. Conductors on the early models had to hop on and off to change the points. The trolley arms clanked as their rattled through the overhead junctions. As the final journey was made in January 1962 you might just be looking at the funeral procession of the last trolleybus in Barnet.

Top: This London Transport trolleybus was the first to roll along Barnet's High Street. During 1936-37 the trams were phased out. Their tracks would be ripped up and some of the scrap recycled during the war to help build tanks and destroyers. The buses that replaced the trams that had been in operation since the early years

Above: It was early in January 1962 and the Christmas lights still shone near the parish church. Winters 40 years ago seem to have been so much harsher than they are today. Maybe there really is a greenhouse effect and our climate is changing. The slush and snow had made the roads slippery for the trolleybus turning the corner. It had just passed through the notorious bottleneck and was making its way along High Street. By the time the truly wicked winter of 1963 arrived this bus had been consigned to the memory banks. It was the lucky one. The rest of us had to suffer the great freeze when rural hamlets were cut off, power lines froze and even professional soccer was put into cold storage. That 1963 winter was the first time the pools panel sat. It forecast the match results so that punters could still lay a bet. Trolleybuses first ran in London in 1931. By July 1936 they were being introduced into Barnet. The trams were phased out as their routes were taken over. The new form of transport still used much of the old overhead cabling to connect the pantographs to the electricity

of the 20th century took over their old routes. They even used the same terminus, near St John the Baptist Church. New terminology came into the language of the transport industry. Frog pulls, power notches and bamboo poles mystified the passengers, but they meant vital equipment to the trolleybus operators. Luxurious Q1 buses and K1 class vehicles made busmen drool. The public was more interested in whether they were on time. The policeman on the corner needed eyes in the back of his head. As he stood on point duty he had to shepherd pedestrians across the road. There were cars heading towards him and a trolleybus bearing down on him from behind. It was a complex job to keep everything flowing smoothly. The change from tram to trolley meant that the war memorial had to be moved into the churchyard. It became hidden from view instead of dominating the High Street corner. Passengers on the top deck of the bus could glimpse it as they looked out. Let us hope they remembered the reason why it had been erected in the first place.

British is best. In the 1960s Brian Poole and the Tremeloes were asking 'Do you love me?' Peter O'Toole was riding a camel in 'Lawrence of Arabia'. Our prime minister at the start of the decade was known as Supermac. Even our criminals were the tops, pulling off a famous £1 million train robbery in 1963. British cars rolled along the roads, none more popular than the remarkable Mini.

First produced in 1959 by the British Motor Corporation, it was the brainchild of designer Alex Issigonis. It was introduced in response to the 1956 Suez energy crisis and the popularity of Germany's Volkswagen Beetle. Despite being only 10 feet long its practicality and affordability made it immediately popular. The Mini is heading towards us from Wood Street, on the left. Waiting to the right would have

been traffic ready to come through The Squeeze, as this part of High Street became known because of its narrow carriageway. An old market building used to obscure this view of St John the Baptist. It later became a baker's shop, but was destroyed by fire in 1899. Traffic has flowed, or more recently crawled, along this stretch of the Great North Road since the Middle Ages. The importance of the route put Barnet

on the map. In 1249 the existence of East Barnet was recorded. As traffic increased it was necessary to differentiate between this settlement and what became known as Chipping Barnet by 1329. By 1347 tolls were being collected to maintain the road from St Albans to Finchley. The streets here were no picture postcard. They were dirty and dusty, covered with animal droppings and dung heaps.

Right: The people on the embankment had come to pay their last respects. Even though it was a wet and wintry day in February 1952 the largely female onlookers had stood waiting patiently for the locomotive to pass by. Headscarves were pulled tight, fur coats buttoned and brollies held high as the funeral train went through. It was carrying the remains of King George VI. He had died peacefully in his sleep at Sandringham. At last he was at rest. The King was just turned 56. He had been catapulted into the limelight when his brother abdicated in 1936. For a shy man, troubled by an unfortunate stutter, it was not a role he relished. Fortunately, he was supported by the strong woman we came to know with affection in later years as the 'Queen Mum'. While his body lay in state in Westminster Hall some 305,806 people filed past to say farewell to the man who had shared the troubles of war and peace with them. His mother, Queen Mary, cut one of the saddest figures at his funeral. He was the third of her sons to die. It is an awful thing for a parent to lose a child. To outlive three offspring is more than the heart can bear. Maybe that was the reason for such a strong female representation on the embankment as the train went by. They could appreciate the loss a grieving mother would feel. The locomotive sounded a single, solemn whistle to acknowledge their condolences.

Bottom: East Barnet Road becomes known as Station Road once it reaches the bridge at New Barnet. The bus is headed in that direction. The population of the parish of East Barnet was just 851 in 1861. The 1871 census put it at nearly 3,000. Another 1,000 were added by 1881. The arrival of the railway had its effect in attracting house builders to develop the area for the rail users who could now access the city centre and other suburbs so much more easily. East Barnet has always been proud to let other Barnets know that it is the earliest of them. The mother church of the whole district was established here. St Mary the Virgin dates from c 1100. East Barnet's history was reflected in the coat of arms of the old Urban District Council. The main motif was the Battle of Barnet, but the gold fleur de lys refers to the parish church. The mum wheeling her pram along the pavement in 1951 was not too interested in heraldry. She was more concerned that the government had just sliced twopence off the weekly meat ration. That meant about four ounces per person. Butchers estimated that it would take 13 ration books to buy a leg of lamb. The war had been over for nearly six years. Is this what her father had died at El Alamein for? She had voted in Mr Attlee and his Labour Government to improve her lot. In October she decided enough was enough. Her cross was written against the name of Churchill and the Conservatives.

Shopping spree

Before the days of motorways, major trunk roads and various bypasses changed the numbering of our roads and the direction of long distance traffic, High Street was part of the A1, the Great North Road. This section is at the Hadley end of the town. It was near Hadley that the Battle of Barnet took place. On Easter Sunday 1471 one of the most important conflicts of the Wars of the Roses took place. Later battles would be held with the traffic that clogged the A1 that was supposed to move it along efficiently. When new roads and traffic systems came along this highway was renumbered as the A1000. It was an unusually quiet day when this photograph was taken. The man waiting to cross the road only had a cyclist to contend with. In later years he would have plenty of time to stand and wait for a gap in the traffic

to appear. The crossing he was using was part of a set of measures brought in by a government alarmed at the rising tide of fatalities on the roads. On 28 March 1934 a comprehensive set of measures to improve road safety was included in the Road Traffic Bill. All new drivers had to take a driving test. Pedestrians could be prosecuted for walking dangerously. Speed limits were imposed in towns. Plans were made to copy a successful Parisian experiment with pedestrian crossings. Leslie Hore-Belisha was the minister of transport given the job of overseeing the changes. He was the Secretary of State for War when hostilities broke out in 1939. However, it is with the flashing beacons that stand by the first crossings he introduced that his name has forever been linked. The black and white markings on the roadway did not come until 1951.

The parade of shops looks almost exactly the same today as it did in 1933. Only the circular centrepiece of the roof facade has gone. Everything else is untouched. John Swain and Son Ltd erected the High Street building at the start of the 1930s. Bath Place is just to the left of the parade. The shops stand on the site of the land once known as Mary Payne's Place. Weekly markets were once held there. By the time this scene was captured Barnet folk could do their shopping here under cover. The saddler's shop, to the right, is a reminder that the days of true horsepower were still important for some. Petrol and diesel engines had not taken over completely, though those days were not too far away. The shop is now called Candles Corner. This corner of Barnet was often used as a hiding place for shoppers when the cattle market was in full swing. It was held not far from Mary Payne's Place, just a stone's throw away on St Albans Road, or New Road as it was called until 1937. Farmers used to drive cattle in from the farms to the north of Barnet and even from as far afield as Wales. Instead of turning the corner here towards the market some beasts tried to make good their escape by continuing down High Street. People were glad of doorways and alleyways in which to dodge out of harm's way.

Above: It was all very well pushing a bicycle down the middle of the road in 1954. Try doing today what the man on the right was doing on his way towards the bridge over East Barnet Road. He was headed west, towards Station Road. The road markings had only been there since 1951. That was when safety experts decided to do something more about cutting the number of deaths on our roads. The pedestrian crossings, introduced 20 years earlier, had helped. Even so, there had been a large number of accidents on them in the immediate postwar years. Drivers argued that they did not easily spot the Belisha beacons. They were too busy concentrating on the road. Pedestrians were lulled into a false sense of security. Some seemed to imagine that an invisible barrier would protect them if they just stepped out into the road in front of the beacon. A compromise was found. Those on foot were encouraged to stop, look and listen as they did at level crossings. White rectangles were painted onto the black tarmac to warn drivers. The pattern they created quickly put 'zebra crossing' into the English language. The scene at this corner has changed little. There are offices on the first floor of the row, but the shops remain.

Above right: Building Woolworth's began in 1933. By 1936 it was well established at 136-138 High Street. The American experience had arrived in Barnet. Despite its transatlantic roots, the store settled into the British way of life quite happily. Perhaps it was because it was cheap and cheerful, rather than loud and brash. The original five and ten cent store adopted British coinage in its adverts. Frank Winfield Woolworth opened his first outlets in 1879 in New York and Pennsylvania. Within 10 years he had opened 22 more.

Success upon success followed. His empire crossed the big pond in 1909 and arrived in Liverpool. Within 25 years Woolworth was a household name in this country. Not only that, it became a much loved establishment, with its own peculiar style of shopping. It became fun to choose sweets from the pick 'n' mix trays. Little liquorice fish, fruit drops and sherbet counters could be dropped into paper bags, each trying to outdo the other for the right to tickle the taste buds. Cheap LP records appeared on the racks. They offered cover versions of hits of the day. It was expensive to buy 12 singles of top 20 hits. The songs were all there on one record for a fraction of the price. Unfortunately the quality of the recordings was often tinny and the singers and musicians not quite up to producing an accurate copy. Perhaps it would have been better to save up for the real thing after all. One of life's great mysteries has never been answered. Why did Woolie's shop assistants always ask customers, 'How much is it, love?' when they brought a purchase to the till for payment.

The drug store and the International Stores next door give this 1936 picture an almost transatlantic feel to it. But, do not be alarmed. The Americans had not taken over the High Street. Parkes made sure that the shop still retained the words 'chemist' and 'pharmacy' on its frontage. We are still more familiar with those descriptions of the business that sold Carter's Little Liver Pills and Andrews' Liver Salts. They were dispensed to those who had stayed too long at the Star Hotel next door. Mums used to go to Parkes to get the awful cod liver oil that was spooned into the mouths of so many protesting children. It tasted so foul that it had to do us some good. Why else would we have been made to suffer? The taste lingered for ages. Parkes eventually gave way to another chemist. Timothy White and Taylor's, a big rival of the Boots empire, appeared in its place. Today the shop belongs to Robert Dyas, ironmonger. A medical link with the past has been kept in the adjacent premises of the International Stores. It is now Specsavers. The chap bending over the contraption at the side of the kerb was not some sort of barrel organ player. He was a knife grinder. The sparks flew from his wheel as he sharpened the blades that people brought to him. He did not limit himself to knives: axes, lawn mower blades and scythes were all the same to him. However, you had to wait until he called round to the house or farm. It was not recommended that you walked down High Street brandishing a sickle!

Bottom: J Sainsbury is now a major player in the cut-throat supermarket industry, with wider links in DIY and garden centres. The company also has interests overseas, in France and the USA. Even when this picture was taken on 25 September 1980 Sainsbury's had branched out into petrol stations, hypermarkets and had become a plc. This store was to close in two days' time. Shoppers were in a hurry to snap up last minute bargains before the awnings were pulled down for the last time and the company left this spot on Barnet's High Street where it had stood for over half a century. It had helped introduce the British to self service in stores. The practice came into being during the 1950s. Although we were kidded that it was for our convenience it was really to help shops increase trade and profit. Shops were able to have a greater number and variety of goods on display. Sainsbury's even produced adverts entitled 'How to shop self service'! As they crossed the road to get their groceries people in this photograph were chatting about Prince Charles' latest girlfriend. Pictures of a teenaged nursery assistant, Diana Spencer, had appeared in the national press. Unwisely photographed in a see through skirt, this innocent looking young girl would eventually win the hearts of the nation as the much loved Princess of Wales. Elsewhere in the world Iraq was at war with Iran. Closer to home, John Arlott, veteran cricket commentator, gave his last ball by ball description of Test match action.

Right: There really was a time in Sainsbury's and other stores when you could get your groceries over the counter. Shop assistants actually passed the time of day with you as well as weighing out the cheese and passing over the pots of jam. Nearly every town in England has a branch of Sainsbury's, but in its early days the company mainly served the London area. The first shop was opened by John James

and Mary Ann Sainsbury at 173 Drury Lane. They sold butter, milk and eggs. He had begun work at 14, working in a grocer's shop near Waterloo. Mary worked in her father's dairy shop. Little did they realise that their little enterprise would turn into a multi million pound empire. A second shop was added in Kentish Town in 1873. Although other branches followed, Sainsbury's did not fully develop the full range of the grocery trade until after World War I. Still concentrating on the south of England, the first branch in the Midlands did not open until 1936. People with a keen eye for detail might spot that Sainsbury's stores were quite often sited in the middle of a parade of other shops. This was quite deliberate. Away from the corner of a street the centre shops did not suffer from the dust thrown up by horse drawn vehicles as they negotiated the bend. Corner shops also had more windows. As well as having less wall display space, the interiors were not as cool as those of their neighbours. This was an important factor in the days before refrigeration. Sainsbury also realised that a central position made for easier expansion into adjacent property.

Making a living

As smart a set of lads as you could imagine posed outside High Barnet Fire Station in 1940. On closer examination this fine body of men included some who could no longer be described as lads. Some of the younger fire officers had joined the armed forces and were serving overseas. Men who might have seen action in the first world war filled their ranks. The first fire brigade in the area was a volunteer force, formed in 1870. Based at 3 Hope Villas, East Barnet Road it used a horse-drawn hand pump, mounted on a small cart. A second brigade was added in 1890 when High Barnet was served from a station in High Street. It was to close in 1948. By the time of this photograph the fire service had the use of the very best of modern equipment. It was to need it. During the days of the Blitz the men were hard pressed to deal with the fires that raged throughout the borough. Without a thought for themselves they risked life and limb rescuing residents trapped in their houses. As they turned their hoses on the flames licking around them they were in constant danger from falling masonry. All the while bombs rained down around them. Their colleagues may have gone off to fight a war abroad, but these brave souls fought just as fiercely on British soil. Their job was not to keep the home fires burning, but to put them out.

Above: Barnet still has its Odeon Cinema at the junction of Station Road and the A1000. Its other main cinema was known as the Gaumont. It closed in August 1959 and was demolished two years later. Before 1955 it was called the Barnet Cinema, also being known as the Cinema Palace in its earlier days. The High Street fire that engulfed it, 20 years before it became the Gaumont, would not have cost Barnet Press anything in travel expenses for its reporters. The printing offices were but yards away. Barnet Press had been founded by George W Cowing (1835-89) in June 1859. Like so many businesses, it had humble origins. George, in concert with brother Charles, bought a secondhand press for £130 and installed it in the garden shed. It was a considerable investment, worth about £8,000 in today's figures. Although there was some competition from the Barnet Advertiser, later the Gazette, soon Barnet Press had the field to itself. By 1889 George's widow was in charge. E Cowing and Son, as the company owner became known, referred to her and son Leslie. The staff used to have a regular printers' outing that became known as a 'Wayzgoose'. This was supposed to hark back to an occasion when those on the trip had an especially fine meal of goose. The fire certainly cooked the cinema's goose. It had to be rebuilt. A Bud Flanagan and Chesney Allen film released the same year was called 'A Fire Has Been Arranged'. No one suspected that Barnet Press had anything to do with this one, but it came in handy!

Right: The funeral cortege stretched back along High Street from the junction with New Road (St Albans Road) towards Monken Hadley, where the force was based. The dull, rainy day seemed to add to the sombre mood of the proceedings. Last respects were being shown to Chief Officer CF Norton. He had been the leading figure in the fire brigade that had progressed from using horse drawn carts to being equipped with the best Leyland machines that money could buy. Before the first world war firefighters had to make do with a steam fire engine. Many of the men were volunteers and sometimes soldiers were enlisted to help out. Boys were used to run to fire officers' homes or places of work to call them out to attend to an incident. Not until 1913 were call bells fitted to their houses. A hooter was used as backup to call in the part timers. The helmets the men wore changed little in basic design during the first quarter of the 20th century. They kept heads safe from falling debris and looked very smart on ceremonial occasions. During the 1930s things changed. The fine brass helmets were done away with. It was discovered that they tended to light up and turn the men's hair frizzy when they came into contact with electric cables! Firefighting had come a long way from dealing with hayricks and thatched roofs in rural areas. There were more hazards to fighting a fire than just dealing with the flames.

Work on the replacement bridge at New Barnet carried on as steam locomotives thundered by. In the 1930s our successors to Stephenson's Rocket were amongst the best in the world. The 1932 Cheltenham Flyer achieved 81.6 mph on a 77 mile journey. In 1934 on St Andrew's Day, appropriately, the Flying Scotsman averaged over 97 mph between London and Leeds. The following year saw the 100 mph barrier broken on the London-Newcastle run and by LNER's Silver Jubilee express. In 1937 the Coronation Scot reached Edinburgh from London in a record breaking six hours. But the most memorable of all achievements came on 3 July 1938.

The Mallard, a streamlined Gresley A4 Pacific, was clocked at 126 mph at Peterborough on the LNER line. The proud designer, Nigel Gresley, was on board to enjoy the moment. He gave his name to one of the many fine machines that used to pull trains under New Barnet Bridge. It was the golden age of steam. Oldtimers used to say that it was quicker to travel to King's Cross from Barnet by loco than it ever became in the 1980s and 1990s. This general view of the work on the new bridge was taken in June 1936. Although it looked as though a bomb had hit it, the site would soon take on some sense of order. The cranes lifted the new sections into place and things ran smoothly once more.

THE BOROUGH OF BARNET *Memories*

Below: We do like to watch people at work. There is something quite satisfying about observing others sweating away in the height of the summer as we idly stand around. The fascination for the onlookers in 1936 lay in the approaching completion of the bridge over East Barnet Road. The station yards at New Barnet were home to various coal merchants and fruiterers. They had depots into which goods and produce could be offloaded before being moved off elsewhere on the backs of lorries. They headed for market, the shops or our own homes. Piles of sand, cement, bricks, tiles and slates stood high, waiting to make similar journeys. Even goods for major stores like Woolworth's came through these yards. A cattle dock was located adjacent to Lancaster Road. When the time came around for Barnet Fair to be held herds of animals were delivered in rail trucks and driven on foot to Barnet. Station Road was like a scene from an Oregon cattle drive. Pigeon fanciers brought their birds in cages and

released them from the side of the tracks. They covered the sky with their wings and the ground below with something less pleasant. The station used to hold special open days. Handsomely styled blue trains would be on show. Traders and businesses set up stalls to advertise the services they could offer. There were sideshows with roll a penny, hoopla and coconut shies. The show on offer on this day was free as the girders were swung into the right position.

Bottom: Construction was underway on 28 June 1936. The station at New Barnet was the first one to be opened in the town. Over the years money was pumped into it. In 1989 it was badly hit by fire. Rebuilding, at a cost of £200,000, took until 1993 to complete. Earlier, in the mid 1970s, full electrification of the line meant a costly revamp. It included replacing the old footbridge over the station that was suffering from metal fatigue. The bridge in this picture had been an old brick

arch. By replacing it with a metal one road traffic could pass more easily underneath. East Barnet Road had become busier as more vehicles struggled to make their way out towards Cat Hill. The bridge almost acted as a social border. On its Station Road side the houses were quite smart and comfortably sized. East of the bridge the properties were generally smaller and less elegant. There were also numerous shops and little businesses dotted along the road. A historical spin-off from the digging was made early that autumn. One of the workmen digging up the road discovered an old sword. It was thought by some to be over 2,000 years old.

High-flying bobbies

Many of us still cheerfully refer to police officers as 'Bobbies'. That nickname is of course derived from Sir Robert Peel who in 1829 formed the first paid, full time uniformed police service when as Home Secretary he succeeded in getting his Metropolitan Police Act through Parliament.

In the early days of the Metropolitan Police recruits had only a three week course of foot drill before being posted to divisions where they learned their real duties from older and more experienced colleagues.

From 1869 divisional 'school-master' sergeants put recruits through their early training - a far cry from today's professional tuition at the Hendon Police College. It was only in 1907 that the first organised training school was opened at Peel House, in London's Regency Street: by the outbreak of the first world war the course there lasted eight weeks . During the 1914-18 war both recruitment and training however were suspended and Peel House was used as a club for overseas troops.

After the Great War several auxiliary buildings were used for police training but Peel House remained the centre with the initial course extended to 10 weeks in 1927. Peel House would be run in parallel with the Metropolitan Police training school at Hendon for many years before finally closing its doors in 1968.

Lord Trenchard the 'Father of the RAF' became Commissioner of the Metropolitan Police in October 1931. The Police College was probably the most controversial of his reforms, initiated because of his concerns about leadership.

When he founded the Force Sir Robert Peel had ruled that promotion should come from within the service. A Royal Commission on Police Powers and Procedures had however reported in 1929

Above: The original 'Peelers'.

1910 that Louis Bleriot the French aviator, who in July 1909 had become the first man to fly the English Channel, opened the site as Hendon Airfield.

In December of 1910 Claude Graham-White acquired the airfield, renaming it the London Aerodrome. The £10,000 'Daily Mail' London to Manchester air race was won by a pilot from Hendon. In the summer of 1911 the first air mail was inaugurated between Hendon and Windsor whilst in the years before the outbreak of the Great War Hendon saw three Aerial Derbies as well as races to Paris and back.

The first world war period saw the development of the site and its extension to the north of Aerodrome Road. The estate became the home of Graham-White's flying school and, as more buildings were added, to the Graham-White Aviation Company which after the war formed the London Flying Club which existed until 1921. Today an 8 ft by 12 ft high Portland stone fireplace with iron dogs in the Queen's Room is all that remains of the original buildings.

After attempts to use the estate as a London country club failed the Air Ministry bought the site in 1926. By this time the area north of Aerodrome Road had become a busy RAF station. On 31st May 1934 the then Prince of Wales, yet to gain notoriety through his friendship with Mrs Simpson and eventual

that higher posts should be filled by the best men available irrespective of the source.

This was how Metropolitan Police training first became associated with Hendon. In 1934 to provide facilities for a new training college 1934 the Receiver of the Metropolitan Police purchased the London Flying Club freehold site of more than 68 acres from the Air Ministry. Later additional land would be bought from the London Passenger Transport Board.

The area occupied by the training estate as it exists today is closely linked with the development of aviation. Soon after the turn of the century EI Everett built and flew his own aircraft from a temporary shed on a field between the Midland Railway and Edgware Road. Everett's flying machine ended its maiden flight in a tree and was afterwards referred to as the 'Grasshopper'. It was not however until 1st October

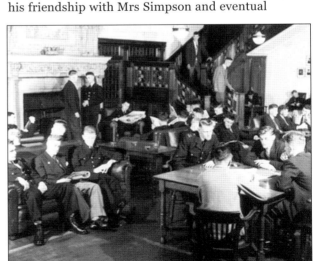

abdication, accompanied by Lord Trenchard laid the foundation stone of 'The New Metropolitan Police Training School'. The original tablet commemorating the event is on display in the Reception foyer today. The foundation stone was however never added to and the Metropolitan Police College was formally opened in buildings which had been the Country Club accommodation.

In May 1934 the first entrants began their 15 months stint of intensive study and practical training (later extended to two years) which included six months on the beat as constables. The college had many opponents, largely because it was felt an officer class would be created and that only men from the upper classes and universities would be accepted. In fact nearly two thirds of the places were reserved for men already serving in the Forces.

In 1935 and 1936 some of the other establishments which today occupy the estate saw their small beginnings. The Driving school and Wireless school for example were officially opened in converted aircraft hangers on 7th January 1935.

The first driving course began in January 1935 when 21 men started a four week course of instruction which included elementary motor mechanics, practical maintenance and driving tuition. In 1936 an advanced course of driving for Flying Squad, 'Q' car and Traffic Patrol drivers was introduced. Motor cycle training was introduce in 1938 The training worked - in 1934 the accident rate for police cars was one per 8,000 miles 40 years later police cars were involved in only one accident per 41,000 miles.

Early in 1936 the training of detective constables commenced in huts which stood at the edge of the sports field. So began the Detective Training School which, after moves to Walton Street in 1961 and Peel

Telecommunications and Management (now Information Technology) Training School. Only three of the original buildings remain, used mainly as stores and workshops.

House in 1968, was finally established in the new classroom block in 1973.

During the second world war Hendon was used as an Army centre for physical education. No police training took place on the estate during the war years; when it restarted in 1946 the training included new recruits as well as detective and driver training - and courses began for overseas police officers.

The second half of the 1960s brought about a complete transformation of the estate which had changed very little over the previous 40 years. The Cadet Corps was formed in 1960 and after first being housed in huts was finally established in its new building in 1968. The building of the three tower blocks, the new classroom block, and the medical centre at the east end of the estate was started at that time. The move into that new accommodation was completed during 1973 and the whole complex was officially opened by Her Majesty the Queen on 31st May 1974, exactly 40 years to the day on which her uncle the Prince of Wales had laid the original foundation stone.

Other major developments during this period included the resiting of the Driving School next to the Cadet School and the building of the Police National Computer Complex between the old and new Driving Schools. The gymnasium/swimming pool/Queen's room complex and reception centre which stand in the site of the original Police College main building were added in the late 1970s. In the early 1980s Farrow House on the other side of the underground line was acquired to accommodate the expanding

The most recent development has been the building of the Training Village which allows training in real life scenarios, where students are assessed and their performances captured on video

Today the Hendon Police College contains many reminders of the history of the Force. A clock for example was retrieved from the old Metropolitan Police Orphanage before its demolition at Strawberry Hill, Twickenham to be placed in the gymnasium. The training school library includes several rare books: one is believed to be the very first instructional book on policing entitled 'Observations on the Office of Constable' written in 1754 by Saunders Welch the High Constable of Holborn.

Perhaps however the most valued reminder of the college's proud heritage is the statue of Robert Peel originally erected in Cheapside in 1855 five years after his death. The statue was later moved to Postman's Park Aldersgate. In 1971 the Court of Common Council of the City of London agreed to give the statue to the Metropolitan Police and it now has a place of honour at the College of the police service he founded.

Above: The Graham White Airfield.
Top right: The statue of Robert Peel.
Right: The Training Village.

Learning to live

'Education, education, education' may well have been one of Tony Blair's electoral warcries but for the people of Barnet that electioneering slogan was nothing new.

In particular Barnet College, the result of a merger between Barnet and Hendon Colleges, can trace one strand of its history back to the times of Elizabeth I.

Prior to their merger, Barnet and Hendon Colleges constituted the two centres of Further Education within the Borough, Hendon serving the south and west and Barnet the north, east and south-east.

Hendon College was formed in 1973 when the Higher Education work of the former Hendon College of Technology went into the Middlesex Polytechnic. At that time it had a site in the centre of Hendon which it vacated on taking over the Grahame Park site in 1986.

Queen Elizabeth I granted Robert Earl of Leicester a charter in 1573 to build a Grammar School in Barnet. As a consequence the site of Barnet College's Tudor Hall was bought and a building erected around 1577.

The history of Barnet College is however much more complicated than simply the story of just one of the many buildings it occupies.

The inhabitants of Barnet could attend lectures provided by the Barnet Institute from 1841 but it was not until 1889 that the Barnet Centre for the London Society for the of the Extension of University Teaching started: in 1889 there was a course of ten lectures on English Literature held at the Boys' Grammar School.

In 1892 the London Society was amalgamated with the Barnet Technical Instruction Committee becoming the Barnet University Extension and Technical Instruction Society with eight subjects being taught and 564 students enrolled. Classes were advertised as being suitable for artisans with students of carpentry and plumbing preferred; by 1896 the range of courses had widened to include dressmaking, fruit culture and 'Accidents - How to Treat Them' or 'First Aid' as we

Above left: *Extract from the Manual Training Examination - 1896.*
Above right: *A 19th century schoolmaster!*
Below: *The classrooms of the old school.*

would now say, together with City and Guilds classes in carpentry, mechanical drawing, wood carving, vegetarian cooking and clay modelling whilst the following year, Pitman Shorthand and Laundry made their first appearance.

Under the Education Act of 1902 Technical and Further Education became the responsibility of Local Education Authorities - in this case the Hertfordshire Higher Education Sub-Committee.

His Majesty's Inspectors' Report of 1903/04 recommended the provision of a Barnet Technical Institute, though no immediate result was seen with classes being held in Christ Church Schools, Alston Road, Queen Elizabeth Boys' Grammar School, Wood Street and the Cookery Centre, Byng Road School.

Following the first world war Education Acts provided for the compulsory attendance at Day Continuation Schools by school leavers between the age of 14 and 18 - mass truancy ensured the scheme soon became voluntary.

Above centre: *The Hall in the late 19th century.*
Top: *The Elizabethan (Tudor) Hall.*

In 1930 however it was agreed to buy the Queen Elizabeth Boys' Grammar school building for £3,000 with the school closing there in July 1932.

The County Council purchased the old school buildings including the Headmaster's house but not the Tudor Hall. By December 1933 the six classrooms, a laboratory and a lecture room had been decorated, the wooden buildings re-roofed and a surface water drainage system laid. The chimney stacks on the main block were rebuilt and the electric system remodelled.

Typical classes in that first 1933 term included cabinet making, book keeping mathematics, shorthand, office skills and cooking with fees ranging from 5 shillings (25p) for the cabinet making course to 2 shillings (10p) for the cookery course. In total that year 346 students were registered.

The Butler Education Act became law in 1944 charging local authorities with responsibility for providing facilities for 'full-time and part-time education for persons over compulsory school age' and for 'leisure time occupation in such organised cultural training and

recreative activities as are suited to their requirements for any persons over compulsory school age who are able and willing to profit by the facilities provided for that purpose'. As a result, in December 1945, approval was given to erect a number of County colleges including one at Barnet, with a technical bias.

Despite the urgency, it was not until 16th June 1949 however that the East Barnet Continuation School moved to Wood Street and became the South Hertfordshire Further Education Centre and which also embodied the Barnet Evening Institute.

During 1950, in addition to evening classes, day release students numbered 290 with many larger local firms adopting day release policies, although according to the College Principal there was still a widespread reluctance by many businesses to offer a general scheme of day release to their employees.

That reluctance soon began to be eroded: the following year day release students numbered 358 and by 1952 reached 450 out of a total number of students enrolled of 1,469.

The buildings by that time consisted of the old Victorian block of eight classrooms, the Tudor Hall and the Lodge which contained the administrative offices and two classrooms. In addition evening classes were scattered in class-

rooms and halls throughout Barnet and East Barnet providing for a range of recreational activities such as physical education, ballroom dancing, art, pottery, woodwork and metal work. Examination classes were mainly aimed at RSA qualifications, City and Guilds and AEB General Certificate of Education, all free to students under 18 years of age.

As the College continued to grow, the Wood Street cottages were taken over as additional accommodation and further prefabricated classrooms were erected in a car park area. Although the Victorian buildings were attractive, it was clear that further buildings were

Above: The Hall viewed from the playground.
Below: One of the classrooms.

required especially to provide specialist rooms for technical and commercial subjects. Some of the older property might have to be demolished: fortunately in the course of surveying the site in the late 1940s the County Architect Charles Aslin had noted the poor state of one important relic from earlier times - the mulberry tree reputed to be 300 years old still bearing fruit and having well outlived the buildings behind it.

In April 1953 the LEA accepted a recommendation for a change of title to the South Herts College of Further Education and at the same time plans were drawn up for a new building to provide new workshops, a drawing office and laboratories. The College had established its role as a training provider and in 1952 the Principal reported that 33 employers were by then sending day release students, the largest groups coming from Standard Telephones and Cables (107 boys and 117 girls), Eastern Electricity Board and John Laing & Son.

There was great pressure to start on the expansion and building was due to commence in 1954 with the aim of having laboratories, workshops, drawing offices, classrooms, library and canteen ready for 1956. The library is believed to have been the first technical library in a further education college in the country. Due to delays, however, the official opening of the new wing was delayed until the Summer of 1957.

The early 1960s had seen the establishment of the Borehamwood annexe as a separate college - and the appearance for the first time of the name 'Barnet College' following a renaming in September 1963. The separation of Borehamwood resulted in the diversion of most general classroom provision to that site and the rapid development of that college contrasted with the delays in planning and completion of the new building of the congested Wood Street site.

Above left: *Inside the Tudor Hall.*
Below: *Music Lessons in the 1970s.*
Bottom: *The Wood Street cottages.*

In a period when some of the other North London colleges were vying with one another over the setting up of the Middlesex Polytechnic, Barnet College appeared to be on the fringe both geographically and 'politically'.

Pointers to future areas of growth, however, lay in the increasing need for second-chance GCE A levels and a steady demand for secretarial studies. There were still major employers committed to sending apprentices to the College, and the launch of the Foundation Art course and courses in collaboration with the Mill Hill Institute took the College into new areas of work where there was no local competition. Given the nature of the Wood Street site, accommodation was still a major preoccupation.

Car parking remained a serious problem which would not be resolved until the council purchased the orchard garden of 27 High Street to turn into a public car park and credited the College with some of the spaces.

The new Phase 3 building took place in 1973 and 1975; by then mobile units had been pressed into service on both the Wood Street and Victoria Road sites and several other temporary premises were in use.

Above centre: *The Wood Street Centre.*
Top left: *An external view of the Hall today.*
Top right: *Graseby House.*

The building at 27 High Street continued to play its part until the 1990s and the decayed grandeur of its rooms and the eccentric character of its heating and plumbing will be forever recalled by the students and staff who spent time there.

Tudor Hall, too, had been a rather decayed condition when taken over by the College in 1965. In 1968 it was completely remodelled to provide teaching and office space whilst still retaining its essential character. Another purchase, in 1973, was the Stanhope Road Centre which was taken over when responsibility for the Adult Education classes taking place there were transferred to the College.

Demand for vocational training and recessional courses and the increase in Day Release by firms meant ever increasing demand and ever increasing student numbers. By 1974 15,000 students were enrolling each year and being offered by then, amongst other facilities, a library with 20,000 volumes, a refectory, common room and bookshop.

Completely new areas of educational provision were opening up in the 1970s such as the development of Flexistudy. Perhaps most significantly was a new venture dating from 1969 when the College became one of the first to offer the new GCE A level in Computer Science, although at that time computers were far too expensive for the College to actually own one itself - students had to trek down to Hendon

Wood Street, the first local authority crèche in Barnet.

Town Hall by bus on Fridays mornings to try their hand at programming using FORTRAN. Whatever happened to those steam driven main frame computers one wonders?

It was not until 1975 that the College was able to obtain its own computer, a second hand ICL 1901A a bulky machine which occupied the largest room available and which used punched paper tape for its input.

Both Barnet and Hendon Colleges developed rapidly through the 1980s for example both acquiring additional sites. Hendon College took over the Grahame Park site between Mill Hill and Colindale; it was a former secondary school which since its acquisition has undergone a £7 million building programme; elsewhere in Hendon, Montagu Road is a former junior school featuring late Victorian architecture.

Nothing ever runs smoothly however. In 1982 a boiler burst in the library block at Wood Street, placing the ground floor under several inches of water, destroying the parquet floor. The same building suffered from a fire in 1991 which, due to prompt action, fortunately caused relatively little damage.

By the time of the 1982 flood, the College was again over-crowded. Southshaw Girls School in East Barnet, dating from the 1930s, was offered as yet another annex. The offer was accepted and a net gain of space was made even though as part of the package the College was obliged to dispose of 15-17 Wood Street and 27 High Street; the latter was a large detached house opposite the police station which was subsequently demolished; the site was, however, later recovered by the College.

Barnet College gradually took root in Russell Lane and in 1987 made another first when it opened a crèche in

College Concerts which had been held for many years in College Hall and Tudor Hall ended in 1995 due to fluctuating support. Later that year, Graseby House was opened. The whole development cost £2.3 million and stands on the spot on which 27 High Street had formerly been.

Many thousands of readers of this book will have attended Barnet and Hendon Colleges at different stages of their lives, for example as young apprentices studying for their City and Guilds qualifications or perhaps as mature students seeking to expand their skills in different areas of life. The new Barnet College, combining the best of two traditions, is today committed to lifelong learning, giving everyone in the community the opportunity to enter or return to education.

Education and how to get one is a critical factor in the development of every community. In the borough of Barnet the words 'Education, education education' really are nothing new, they've been around for generations.

Above left: *An aerial view of the Wood Street Centre in 1980.*
Above right: *Graseby House accommodation.*
Below (left): *John Skitt, Principal since 1985.*
Below(right): *Tony Alderman, Chair of the College Corporation.*

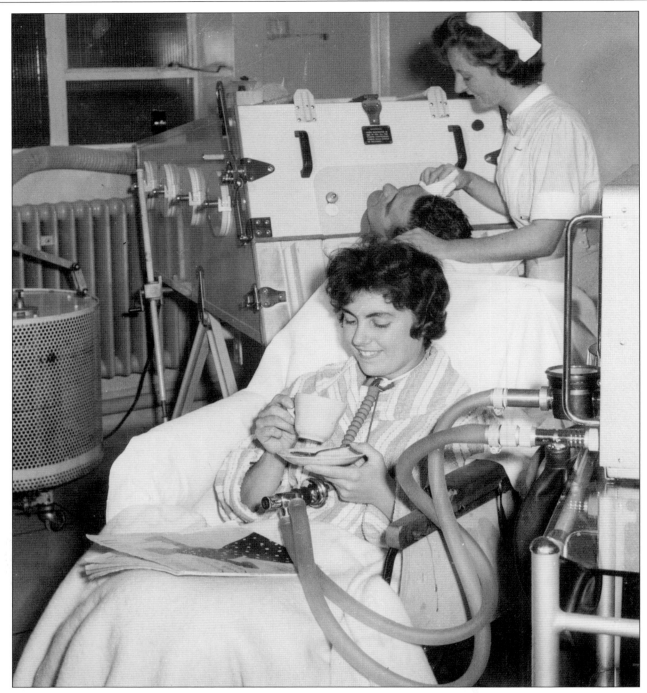

Barnet General Hospital developed as a large spread of buildings with their roots in the workhouse days of the 1830s. What had been the old Barnet Union Wellhouse also incorporated an infirmary. A new one was built in 1895 to help cater for tuberculosis sufferers. The large number of casualties from World War I encouraged more building to take place. In between the world wars other wards and a nurses' home had been added. When the hospital joined the NHS on 5 July 1948 it changed its name to throw off the stigma of the past. By then the polio epidemic was sweeping the country. Known as 'the crippler' the infectious disease affected 7,000 in 1947, killing 700 and leaving many more suffering severe paralysis. Children were particularly vulnerable. The effects of polio were made worse as it affected respiration, making breathing difficult. Philip Drinker's 'iron lung' was a boon to polio sufferers. As the government dithered in the mid 1950s about introducing the Salk vaccine, the mechanical breathing device saved many lives. It was also helpful for those hit by pneumonia. The General Hospital has its own place in this aspect of medical history. In 1959 use of an electronic breathing machine, the Barnet Ventilator, was pioneered at the hospital by the Bells Hill company, W Watson and Sons. The Oscar winning actress, Elizabeth Taylor, was one of many who benefited from the invention. On 5 March 1961 she was admitted to hospital with acute pneumonia. She was within hours of death. The Barnet Ventilator breathed new life into her lungs for 72 hours until she was able to breathe unaided.

OpTex under the spotlight

How many coveted Hollywood motion picture awards have been brought home to Barnet? The answer, perhaps surprisingly, is 'one at least'. Barnet's unrecognised superstar performer is however neither an actor nor an actress but the New Barnet-based firm of OpTex.

The world of Hollywood with its sunny climate, glamorous movie stars, Cadillacs and swimming pools may seem far removed from Barnet but the local firm of OpTex is at the very heart of the international film and television industry.

Today the OpTex group employs over 70 staff and is divided into several divisions each specialising in a different area of activity which, in total, seem to offer everything that one could possibly want in the field of production equipment for television and film. OpTex Broadcast Sales supplies everything from a single lens adapter ring to a complete filming kit; OpTex Lens Manufacturing - the original core business - designs and supplies lenses specialising in Super-16 primes and zooms; OpTex Broadcast Rentals hires out a huge range of equipment including cameras, lenses, microwave communication links, portable lighting and electrical equipment; OpTex Lighting supplies a complete range of studio and location lighting and also manufactures the firm's world famous Aurasoft lights; OpTex Communications provides telecommunications equipment including portable systems with satellite links; OpTex sales services ensure that every piece of equipment is in perfect condition, OpTex R&D provides a bespoke design service for one of commissions and, lastly, OpTex also provides finance via leasing facilities for broadcast and film equipment. As technology advances, OpTex is now heavily involved in the design and manufacture of high definition lenses for sale and rental.

The company has set up a special sales and rental division to manage the exports of this astounding new technology all around the world.

How on Earth did this hive of activity culminating in one of Hollywood's greatest accolades come in to being? The firm of Optical & Textile Ltd was formed in 1969 by two men, Ron Collins and George Hill. Ron Collins was a freelance cameraman who had begun his career as a messenger boy for Rank Screen Services and had later worked as a cameraman for ten years for British Moveietone; later as a freelance documentary cameraman he specialised using extreme telephoto lenses, mainly for sports coverage in numerous Olympic Games and World Cup football matches.

Below: *Optex exhibits at broadcast exhibitions all over the world.* ***Bottom:*** *The company's staff and directors in its earlier days.*

George Hill was a camera and lens maintenance technician whom Ron Collins had met years earlier.

In 1973 the two men moved into small premises in Barnet from where they began to develop and sell lens adapters, mounts and lens conversions to high powered lenses used for wildlife and sports coverage.

One of the products for which the fledgling company soon became well known was the 'Tamaha zoom', a 16mm zoom lens which OpTex converted to a 35mm format. So high was the demand to rent this lens that the firm was able too take on more staff and invest in the best optical bench equipment available.

During the 1970s many of the big manufactures began to approach OpTex asking it to market their products. Always keen to develop new opportunities the availability of lightweight TV cameras for news coverage as an alternative to bulky film cameras was something the firm quickly exploited during that period.

OpTex moved to larger premises in Victoria Road, New Barnet in the early 1980s which were soon expanded to over 30,000 square feet of space. Further expansion followed in 1997 to accommodate the firm's satellite and terrestrial communications business and its Aurasoft Lighting Division.

It was to Aurasoft lighting that the company would owe its Hollywood award.

The idea for Aurasoft, a virtually shadowless softlight, was conceived in 1981 by the aptly named Derek Lightbody, a well known lighting engineer who had worked for the BBC since its Alexandra Palace days. The idea was to build a light with a special reflector which would act as a diffusing agent. The fundamental principle was to build a single reflector consisting of thousands of tiny spheroidal convex mirrors which would reflect light from the lamp in all directions. The result would be a true softlight which would not produce multiple shadows - a light which is the nearest equivalent to natural daylight as possible, casting the same soft shadows as sunlight.

Derek Lightbody had graduated from Leeds University with a degree in Civil Engineering in 1944 and after a period of Naval aviation design joined the BBC as a Radio programme engineer, being involved in orchestral and drama productions until 1949 when he transferred to the BBC's outside broadcast team as a sound and vision engineer. Derek eventually became head of BBC lighting in 1961.

By 1988 however Derek was working on behalf of OpTex in Budapest advising on the development of a high powered multi-source light. In 1991 Derek Lightbody took the Aurasoft to OpTex which provided the resources to develop the concept, turning a vision into reality. Aurasoft had its official launch two years later with the world-wide sales programme beginning in 1995.

Since first going into production the Aurasoft light has been continuously modified to improve its performance and is now in its fourth series.

Every cameraman who has used the Aurasoft Luminaire has loved it; the lights have now been used on such sets as the latest James Bond movie, Trainspotting and Shakespeare in Love.

Top: *Ron Collins (right) and Derek Lightbody receiving the Academy Award for the Aurasoft.*
Above centre: *Three early catalogues of the company's products.*

and Engineering Award. Derek Lightbody, Ron Collins and George Hill were present to receive the award presented by Ann Heche star of such films as Psycho and Six Days, Seven Nights.

At the beginning of the new millennium the small business formed by Ron Collins and George Hill is now a phenomenon: the company has a fleet of purpose built satellite uplink vehicles which can travel anywhere in Europe to provide satellite links to get live news pictures back to broadcasters in the least possible time. As well as vans, the company also provides portable 'flyaway' satellite communication equipment which can be flown as cargo to any part of the world.

Already the recipient of a Prime Time Emmy Engineering award for the development of the Mini Image Intensifier used in US coverage of Desert Storm, OpTex was now nominated for the greatest tribute of all.

It was on 27 February 1999 that the Academy of Motion Picture Arts and Sciences held its 71st Annual academy Award Ceremony at the Regent Beverly Wiltshire Hotel, Beverly Hills, California. For the very first time a British Company was awarded a Scientific

Top: The OpTex showroom is fully equipped for customer demonstrations. Above: One of the uplink vehicles from OpTex's Communications fleet.

Communications are however just one component of this remarkable company. Perusal of the OpTex catalogue offers an extraordinary insight into the working of the film and television industry. Anyone wanting to make a film will find quite literally everything short of actors in the OpTex catalogue, not only camera, lenses, lights and sound recording equipment but everything else too, all the way from clapper boards to location tee shirts.

'Build a better mousetrap and the world will beat a path to your door' Nothing illustrates that old maxim better than the progress made by OpTex in the years since its founding.

Inspired to shop

The faces of our towns and cities change constantly. Sometimes that change is rapid, at other times so gradual that we hardly notice that it is taking place until one day we look at a view familiar from our childhoods and suddenly realise that the whole scene has altered. One of the curiosities of getting older ourselves is the shock of realising that what we personally took to be brand new is now a building which was not built just last year or 'a few years back' but has been there for so long that young children of secondary school age take it for granted that the object of our contemplation has always been there.

At last! The shopping complex that we've all been waiting for

The word 'chipping' in Chipping Barnet actually means market. The town received its charter to hold a market as long ago as 1199 and has had shopping centres of one kind or another ever since. In the 1960s, 1970s and 1980s councils across Britain were gripped with an enthusiasm for building new shopping centres in an echo of the 19th century boom in building covered market halls. Barnet was no exception to the rule.

1989 was a landmark year: in Japan Emperor Hirohito had died, in Iran the Ayatollah Khomeini had issued the famous Fatwa or death sentence against author Salman Rushdie for his book The Satanic Verses, whilst in China the world witnessed the massacre of students in Peking's Tiananmen Square.

Nearer to home The Spires Shopping Centre opened in High Street, Barnet. It provided the population of Barnet and its environs with a much needed prestigious Shopping Centre ideally situated in a prime position at the heart of Barnet and easily accessible from the M25, fulfilling the needs of a busy and growing borough.

Howards' Way star, Jan Harvey, together with the Mayor of Barnet, Dot Benson, performed the opening ceremony in September 1989. After having both arrived at the new centre in a stagecoach drawn by four white horses and being received by the Potters Bar Band Ms Harvey described the new building as 'heaven under one roof'.

Built at a cost of £25 million the centre was jointly developed by Lovell Developments Ltd and Norwich Union. The architects were the firm of Essex, Goodman and Suggitt working in conjunction with designers David Davies Associates.

A Waitrose supermarket provided an 'anchor' for the whole Centre, guaranteeing a steady flow of traffic throughout the development and answered a pressing local need for a large premium food store with easy access to parking.

The Spires takes its name from the remaining spires of the old Methodist Church which once stood where the Centre now stands. The foundation

Above: *The opening of the Centre in October 1989.*
Below: *The Centre's courtyard under construction.*
Below left: *The glass-domed mall.*

Roses: the 1471 Battle of Barnet in which the Lancastrian cause finally failed when the Earl of Warwick remembered as 'Warwick the Kingmaker' was defeated and killed. A modern heraldic emblem was designed echoing the area's rich heritage. The same heraldic theme was adopted to provide direction signs throughout the Centre.

stone of the Methodist Church was laid on May 21st 1891 and the building was completed in 1892 at a cost of £5,000. The church's last service was held on 11th October 1987 following which the congregation relocated itself to Barnet Parish Church. The designers of the new Shopping Centre cleverly retained the architectural assets represented by the church's spires and incorporated them into this most modern of buildings.

Perhaps the second most distinctive feature of the Spires is the variegated slate roof in shades of grey. The designers were aware of the importance of design to the success of every retail scheme. The 'graphic identity' of the new Shopping Centre was inspired by an important event in the War of the

The development project produced 92,460 sq ft of new retail space divided into 36 units including a supermarket and a restaurant and was served by a multi-storey car park. Two enclosed malls led onto open courtyards making it possible to create a classical English garden atmosphere at the heart of the project. Specially designed features such as the intricate floor patterns and lighting added to the elegant tone. The Centre was later to be awarded the London in Bloom 'Cleary Trophy' in 1994, 1995 and 1996 as London's most attractive Shopping Centre.

It was not however only the Shopping Centre which received attention from the designers. The car park

too was given considerable thought; particularly attractive was the way shoppers could enter the Spires Centre without having to pass through any dark or unpleasant corridors. The car park in fact received the Secured Car Parks prestigious Gold award introduced by the police and administered by the AA.

This page: *Christmas 1999 saw the appearance of many famous figures, including Gladiator's Vogue who helped stage Gladiator-type events for the local children.*

In May 1992 the sale of the Centre, with five units still unoccupied, was agreed for just £15.5 million leading to at least one letter in the local press suggesting that the Centre was a white elephant which should have never been built - criticism which in turn stimulated protests from others who found the centre an excellent place to shop. What was true was that at least six traders were reported to be getting ready to leave the Centre.

In June 1992 Frogmore Investments acquired the Centre from Norwich Union and its management team embarked upon a re-appraisal of its lettings. WH smith which had been situated in the High Street soon took over Unit 1 which had previously been occupied by Laura Ashley.

Other changes took place: the water fountain and wishing well made their welcome appearance whilst three specialist kiosks were built in the Western Hall. Frogmore Investments completely re-landscaped the courtyards. They removed the large plants which had originally been there and put in smaller plants making it easier for shoppers to walk to and from the shops on either side of the open courtyards; more seating was provided too.

Frogmore investments subsequently sold the Centre to PDFM in 1996, with Chesterton being the Managing Agents. Following the merger of the Union Bank of Switzerland with the Swiss Bank Corporation in July 1998 PDFM became Philips and Drew Fund Management Limited.

Naturally it was not possible to please everyone: some local traders complained at the outset that they had not been allowed to occupy space in the new Centre; other pundits complained about the traffic being generated or feared that the Centre would be unviable, noting that a number of shop units remained unlet.

Certainly there was some cause for concern: nine months after the opening date only 26 of the 36 shop units had been let.

Above: *The certificate awarded by the London in Bloom Committee to the Spires in 1999.*
Below: *Part of the Christmas 1999 celebrations.*

LONDON in *Bloom*

This certificate was presented by the
LONDON IN BLOOM COMMITTEE
in recognition of the efforts made
in encouraging excellence of
floral display in London

Cleary Trophy 1999

1st Prize

The Spires Shopping Centre

London Borough of Barnet

Date: 29th September 1999

Chairman
London in Bloom

Berkeley HOMES   brophy

The Royal Horticultural Society, Thames Water, The Worshipful Company of Gardeners, The Metropolitan Public Gardens Association McDonald's Restaurants Ltd, Tidy Britain Group, Brophy Grounds Maintenance, Berkeley Homes, Floranova and R.A. Meredith & Son.

Although some tenants did leave others however took their place and business picked up to a point where in 1995 despite two empty units the owners were considering extending the Spires Centre by building three additional units, although those plans were later shelved in the face of public opposition to the expansion, not least the removal of the much loved if little used bandstand.

Despite the prophets of doom the Spires Centre continues to thrive, more popular now than ever with more than 60,000 people visiting it each week.

For those who are alive when a new building is completed it often is difficult to grasp how much it, and its subsequent history, is part of the history of the town. But history is frequently the story of things which have happened in our own lifetimes, not just those of our forebears. In truth even the most ancient of buildings: castles cathedrals and Victorian market halls were once brand spanking new; those who saw them rise from the ground in their youth must have had difficulty in coming to terms with the fact that by their later years, these edifices had already become part of the never ending story of Britain. Modern history, no matter how modern, is still history. The Spires Centre is very much part of the story of our borough. The church which once stood on the site was part of the older history of the town, with no-one now able to recall its beginning, though many still able to recall its middle age and senility before its final demise; what generations yet to come will make of it all cannot be predicted but no doubt they too will experience the same emotions, ideas and misconceptions as we do about exactly when history began.

Below: *The Spires from the air.*

In mint condition

Stamping and pressing sounds rather like a medieval torture. In fact it is the main business of Charles Neal & Son (Finchley) Ltd a family run manufacturing company which has built a reputation over many decades for its high quality, competitively priced metal products such as coins, medals, paperweights, costume and precious jewellery, labels and name tags.

Located at the aptly named 'The Mint' in Friern Park, the Neal family business can trace its origins back almost 200 years to a die sinking and tool making business established in London's Clerkenwell district.

Ralph Neal, the grandfather of Peter Neal the firm's present Chairman, purchased that business from his employer in the mid 19th century and changed its name to his own.

The Ralph Neal company is of historic importance in that it once specialised in the production of market tallies. These were stamped metal ticketing devices used in van loading tallies and accounting for empty containers in the great London markets of Billingsgate, Covent Garden and the Borough market.

Ralph Neal traded for many years before eventually retiring in 1913. He had seven sons and three daughters. Four of the sons he left to run the business, the eldest, another Ralph, becoming the senior director. The company continued under this management, working from premises at 19 Percival Street, Clerkenwell.

Around 1930 the company moved its factory to New Southgate, keeping the Percival Street premises as its city office. The recession of the early 1930s was being felt by most industries, particularly engineering, and the Neal company was no exception; but it survived, continuing to strike medals and metal tickets whilst also manufacturing tools and dies.

Peter Neal had wanted to go into engineering when he left school but for family reasons felt that it would be more prudent to start his own tool-making and die sinking business. His father Charles who was nearing retirement left his brothers at Ralph Neal's to help Peter start Charles Neal & Son acquiring rented premises at High Road East Finchley in 1936.

Above left: *Charles Neal, founder.*
Below: *The premises in the 1980s.*

completing the cycle from the founder to his present day descendants.

Charles Neal & Sons Ltd moved to its present freehold premises in Friern Park, Barnet in 1977, since when the business has flourished.

The third generation of Neals to work in the company were Peter Neal's sons Robert Michael and Andrew. Robert trained as a diesinker and engraver and is now and firm's Managing Director though still involved in the design and creation of new products. Andrew Neal worked for a few years in the company as a tool maker but now works for himself whilst his brother Michael, who also trained as a tool maker, now directs the production and marketing side of the business.

In 1936 the company began with hand operated presses and then progressed to belt driven machines utilising an electric motor which turned a shaft from which machines drew power.

The company now has a range of power presses delivering up to 360 tons pressure. Tooling to make the products is made in a tool room equipped with spark erosion and computer controlled machines.

Today's main products are decorative metal stampings encompassing medals, labels, and name plates, jewellery, promotional items and general industrial pressings. Despite fierce competition from the Far East the company aims to keep ahead through its superior design techniques and a constant upgrading of equipment to state of the art technology. Computer modelling and machining linked to sculptural hand

Charles Neal was Chairman of the new company whilst Peter Neal initially managed production within the factory before eventually taking over from his father. Peter's sisters Evelyn and Vera were also involved in the business, working in the office and despatch departments.

The original Ralph Neal business was eventually sold by the remaining brothers to S L Morris who ran it until 1957 at Oakleigh N20 when the business finally failed.

The stock of S L Morris and Ralph Neal dies was purchased and absorbed into the Charles Neal stock

skills give the firm the ability to turn client's ideas and drawings into three dimensional reality with aesthetics as much to the fore as the engineering practicalities.

Above: *Finishing with hand tools.*
Top: *In production at the power presses.*
Right: *Some of today's products.*

Surveying the scene since World War II

MAC Simmonds and DH Brown began the chartered surveyors' firm now known as Simmonds and Partners in July 1946. Both men had served king and country with pride and no little distinction during the war. As with many other men they had to sacrifice the early years of careers that had begun in the late 1930s. The greater needs of the country took precedence. Simmonds had qualified as a chartered surveyor and Brown was a fully fledged architect when they joined forces at Central Chambers, Hendon Central.

Their skills complemented one another as they set off on the difficult road of becoming established in those austere times of postwar Britain. Although not involved with

the fledgling firm, Mr Simmonds' father, CWB Simmonds, was a builder of some repute. Between the wars he was responsible for building many hundreds of houses in the North London area. One of his most impressive projects was at Hendon's Mulberry Close. Luxury flats were built on the site of an old mansion, known as Tenterden Hall, set in an estate overlooking

Hendon Lawn Tennis Club. With the delightful ornamental gardens around, it was a lovely spot to conduct gracious living. The suites were centrally heated and a snip at £110 per annum for a one bedroom flat, rising to £325 for a large five bedroom apartment. That is a snip at today's prices! CWB Simmonds was a founder director of the Abbey Road Building Society we now know as the Abbey National.

It was not a simple matter to start a new business in 1946. Various wartime restrictions were still in force and there was a host of others trying to establish or restart companies as forces' personnel returned to civvy street. However, the two partners persevered. In the beginning it was a small enterprise, certainly for the first nine or ten years.

Everyone pulled his weight, each becoming a jack of all trades. In the early days, as Simmonds and Brown got themselves onto a firm footing, a lot of the business related to surveying war damaged property and requisitioning work carried out on behalf of local government. Gradually, this extended into surveying on the behalf of building societies and

Above left: *CWB Simmonds, father of the founder.*

successful and rapidly growing public quoted company, although the character of the firm remains strictly unaltered.

As the 21st century unfolds it may become necessary to examine the firm's plans for meeting the needs of society in the third millennium. Currently serving the lending institutions, private investor companies and the general public in survey work, Simmonds an Partners is well aware that traditional valuation work may shrink. The changing face of the building societies and the service they provide may see a contraction of valuation business with them. The present links to property management, with the likes of Asda Property Holdings and Bradford Property Trust (BPT), are ripe for expansion. It is in that direction that Simmonds and Partners is likely to focus in the years ahead.

Above left: MAC Simmonds in about 1936. He would have been about 20 years old.
Above right and below: DAK Simmonds as a young boy pictured at Mulberry Close.

other more general work. As the better days of the mid 1950s came along, there was a greater freedom about the nation. Rationing and restrictions disappeared and there was a new mood of optimism in the country. Industry's order books were beginning to fill and a period of nigh full employment was on the horizon. People had money to spend and expansion was everywhere. The firm moved to 6 Watford Way and continued to develop its portfolio of clients. By 1963 it was generating enough work to justify further development and 10 Watford Way became additional office space for Simmonds and Partners.

About this time David Simmonds joined the firm that his father had helped found. David stayed with the practice until his retirement in June 2000. He had seen it continue to diversify its interests. It became more involved with property management, design work in building alteration and property improvement. The supervision of major building repairs became part of its remit whilst continuing with the established service of supplying valuations for mortgage and insurance purposes. Simmonds and Partners offered then, as it does today, a broad spread of professional expertise within the climate of a close personal client relationship. The partnership was acquired in June 1997 by Hercules Property Services and is now part of a highly

Education for all

For over seventy five years 'The Mount School' in Mill Hill has been providing girls with the opportunity to develop educationally and socially. The School motto 'Esse Quam Videri' ('To be, rather than to seem to be') reflects the belief of the School's founder, Miss MacGregor, that the essential components of education include personal development as well as educational excellence.

The School originally started in a house in Highgate in 1925 with 10 pupils. By 1935 a growth in the number of pupils prompted the move to the Grade II listed building in Mill Hill. During the war years the whole school was evacuated to Gloucestershire. When peace was declared, life at Mill Hill resumed under the capable leadership of Miss MacGregor.

The Mount School retained its rural character for many years; as well as the students and staff, goats, rabbits and donkeys were part of the School. Miss Millin, who was appointed Headteacher after Miss MacGregor's retirement, is fondly remembered as well as her constant companion, Moses the cat.

Below: *The school in its entirety.*
Bottom: *A production of 'As You Like It' in 1949.*

By the 1960s demands for space meant that The Mount School could no longer provide accommodation for boarders. Many old girls who visit the School are surprised to see dormitories converted to classrooms. Sadly the animals also could no longer remain at the school.

Above: *Lesson time.*
Top: *A science lesson from the 1950s.*
Above right: *The school today.*

The education system has seen many changes since 1925, particularly the recent introduction of the National Curriculum. The Mount School has ably met all of these new challenges. Today, the School maintains its old-world charm, with a strong belief among staff to educate individuals, providing students with the facilities to achieve high standards in GCSE, A Level and other external examinations. Whilst incorporating national guidelines and standards into the curriculum, the aims of Miss MacGregor to provide an excellent environment for any girl to develop and achieve her full potential are upheld.

Statons - from cottages to country estates

Barnet, Hadley Wood, Totteridge, Brookmans Park and all surrounding areas. Buying a house has long been acknowledged as being amongst the most stressful of experiences we can ever put ourselves through.

It is at that time we need the services of a top-class, reliable estate agent. Statons is just such an agency. Although it has stars from the world of sport and showbiz on its books, it treats every client with the same level of professionalism, discretion and support. Statons make it their job to take the pressures away from clients and support them with a smoothly delivered package that meets their every need.

Nick and Loraine Staton set up their partnership in 1990. It is a highly professional team headed by Nick Staton and is a true team effort. The estate agency has done so well that, by the end of the decade, it had opened three more luxury offices. As well as the original base in Barnet, Statons now has offices in Totteridge,

Brookman's Park and Hadley Wood. In extending its scope the company has been able to develop a wider range of clients to whom it can offer a first-class service. Vendors have access to a larger set of potential buyers and purchasers are able to view a more varied group of properties.

Statons incorporated Blade & Company, a well-established and respected estate agency of many years and has been able to use the experienced links Blade & Company had with the community under the Statons yellow and black colours. It had been at Blade that Nick Staton began his career.

Above: Nick Staton outside the Hadley Parade, Barnet premises in June 1993. *Below:* Statons incorporating Blade, exchanged April 1999 - Totteridge Lane.

Nick and the team have not forgotten their sense of duty to the many communities in which they do business. As well as selling many homes, they support local schools and sponsor a variety of neigh-bourhood events. Fetes, fairs, charity events, the Hadley Wood Association firework display, Barnet Rugby Club and many schools in the areas they cover have all benefited from the interest shown by Statons. The team are encouraged to be positive about closing sales and always achieving the best for their clients. The Staton philosophy has always been that such business has to be conducted in a special Staton way, with courtesy, respect and dignity. The company has built a fine reputation. The highly motivated team continue to offer their clients metic-ulous marketing and the highest level of advertising.

Statons is a combination of first-class experience, out-and-out enthusiasm and hard work. This achieves the best results for its clients, no matter what the market throws at them.

The highly professional team of 25 employees focus on one thing, matching people to homes. Unlike a number of other agencies Statons does not involve itself in the world of mortgage brokering, legal advice or insurance services. This is often a refreshing change to clients who have had previous experience of others whose attention has been distracted from the main aim of the estate agent - it is pure estate agency - finding a buyer for the property. The company has retooled with the latest computerised equipment that speeds up data retrieval, all in the best interests of conducting speedy and fruitful business. As the new millennium began Statons received a Golden Globe Award for its web site.

Above: *Hadley Wood office, 10 Crescent West.*
Top: *Barnet Hadley Green office.*
Right: *Brookmans Park office.*

A brightly decorated float taking part in the celebrations on Station Road on Whit Monday, June 1949.

Acknowledgments

AJB Mussell (Borough Archivist) and the London Borough of Barnet
Andrew Renwick (Curator of Photographs) and the RAF Museum, Hendon
Gillian Gear, D Willcocks and all the unsung heroes of
Barnet Museum, Wood Street, Barnet
Mr & Mrs David Paul

Thanks are also due to
Andrew Mitchell who penned the editorial text and
Steve Ainsworth for his copywriting skills